COMPETENT CREW

FOR NEW CREW AND COMPETENT CREW STUDENTS

FIFTH EDITION

PAT LANGLEY-PRICE & PHILIP OUVRY

EDITED BY CAROLE EDWARDS

ADLARD COLES NAUTICAL
LONDON

Published by Adlard Coles Nautical
An imprint of A & C Black Ltd
38 Soho Square, London W1D 3HB
www.adlardcoles.com

First edition published by Adlard Coles 1985
Reprinted 1986, 1987, 1990
Second edition published by Adlard Coles Nautical 1991
Reprinted 1995, 1997
Third edition 2000
Fourth edition 2004
Fifth edition 2007

ISBN: 9780-7136-8262-5

A CIP catalogue record for this book is available from the British Library.

This book is produced using paper that is made from wood grown in
managed, sustainable forests. It is natural, renewable and recyclable. The
logging and manufacturing processes conform to the environmental
regulations of the country of origin.

Designed by Margaret Brain
Typeset in 9/12pt Myriad-Light

Printed and bound in Spain by GraphyCems

Note: While all reasonable care has been taken in the publication of this
edition, the publisher takes no responsibility for the use of the methods
or products described in the book.

Acknowledgements and photo credits

The editor and publisher would like to thank the following people
and organisations for their help and advice with photos and artwork:
Cornish Crabbers: page 7, 36; Paul Franks: page 12 (centre); Alistair
Garrod: page 8–9; Gill Marine Clothing: page 3; Alison and Peter Noice:
pages 4, 6, 25 (both), 44, 46, 49, 50, 81, 89, 92 (bottom), 103; Hamble
School of Yachting: pages 2; HM Coastguard: page 121; Janet Murphy:
page 74; Steve Richard (www.stephenrichard.co.uk): page 17, 24
(both), 30, 35, 38, 80; Dave Saunders: page 16, 29, 31, 33, 34, 72, 73, 113,
114; David Williams: pages 12 (left and right), 13, 17, 18 (both), 20–1, 26
(both), 27 (both), 32, 42–3, 45 (both), 47, 53, 60, 64, 82, 83 (both), 84 (all
three), 92 (top), 94, 95 (both); Yamaha/Zodiac 96, 97, 104, 105, 108

Grateful thanks to Malcolm Pearson for his advice and the use of
drawings (pages 14, 15, 47, 84, 89) from his book *Reeds Skippers
Handbook for Sail and Power* published by Adlard Coles Nautical.

contents

Introduction iv
1 Going aboard 2
2 Parts of the boat 6
3 Knots and ropework 12
4 Getting ready to sail 20
5 How the boat sails 28
6 Finding the way 42
7 Steering a course 50
8 How to read a chart 54
9 Weather watching 58
10 Rules of the road 70
11 Going into harbour 80
12 Anchoring and mooring 86
13 Flags and sailing etiquette 96
14 Safety afloat 100
15 Emergencies 102
Sailing quiz 116
Answers to the quiz 128
Appendix 1 – Course syllabus 135
Appendix 2 – Glossary 137
Index 154

introduction

Friends have invited you for a sailing weekend – it's an exciting prospect if you haven't been to sea before but it can be a bit daunting. What will I have to do? Do I need to be able to tie knots? What do I wear? Will I be safe? Lots of questions like these may cross your mind – the aim of this book is to give you the background information you will need to make your initial voyages afloat very interesting and enjoyable experiences.

To be a useful crew member you don't need experience when sailing with a good skipper. You just need to listen and learn, and try to act promptly when asked to do something. Being a novice crewmember should be a fun time – you have all the enjoyment of sailing but not the overall responsibility of navigating and managing the boat. Also you will be learning new skills all the time ranging from tying essential knots to preparing meals afloat, taking compass bearings and steering the boat.

You will also learn about sail trim – how sailors make the best use of the wind to speed along – and what to do if you get into a blow and need to slow down a bit. Anchoring and mooring are essential skills to master – you will learn how to choose the best sheltered cove where you can stop for lunch and a swim – the idyllic side of sailing on a hot summer's day.

Of course there is a serious side to sailing. You will have safety briefings and carry out man overboard drills. You will understand about the potential dangers of being out at sea in a small boat and learn the Rule of the Road and how to deal with emergency situations. But once you have some knowledge and skills you will gain confidence which will add to your enjoyment. This is what sailing is all about.

1 going aboard

Your first invitation to go sailing may leave you wondering what clothing and equipment you will need to pack. This chapter will give you a good idea of what to take with you.

What do I need?

First of all you will need a reasonably sized soft bag for all your belongings. A hard suitcase is unsuitable because it will be difficult to store down below.

The first thing to realise is that you are very likely to get wet! So a good set of waterproofs is essential for staying warm and dry in a blow. Your skipper should be able to advise you what you will need – perhaps he or she can lend you a set. If you are not sure that sailing will be for you, try to borrow or buy an inexpensive second-hand set of waterproofs at first. It is a matter of personal choice whether you opt for a one-piece or two-piece suit but if you are going to buy your own, look out for these key features:

- Waterproof and breathable fabric
- Fully-taped seams
- A high collar with a storm chin flap
- A high-visibility, stowable hood
- Heavy duty zips; storm cuffs for wrists and ankles

The suits need undergarments that will spread any sweat accumulations and will still be comfortable next to the skin if water gets

This crew is well dressed for heavy weather and is wearing a lifejacket and harness.

inside. There are lots of good brands to choose from; do plenty of homework.

Dinghy sailors, who are virtually guaranteed to get wet, often wear dry suits which stop water penetration completely – but these can be hot to wear.

If you are just out for the day and the weather is reasonably good then a lightweight wind and waterproof jacket and casual trousers will probably be fine as outer garments – if you have waterproof overtrousers, take those too. Avoid wearing cotton denim jeans as they get stiff and cold when wet. Remember that how ever hot it seems on land, even in summer it will be quite a few degrees cooler on the water and there is the wind-chill factor to consider.

Thin layers of lightweight tops such as micro-fleeces give better insulation than one thick woolly jumper. They dry more easily and take up less room.

Remember that you need to stay comfortable and warm if you are going to enjoy yourself out sailing.

Footwear

You will need a sturdy pair of deck shoes with non-slip, non-marking soles – there are lots on the market – both leather and canvas. Sandals are unsuitable as there are lots of items on deck which you can stub your toes on. If you are going to wear trainers, make sure that they don't have dark soles which may mark the deck.

Other clothing items

Gloves Waterproof sailing gloves give grip on rope.
Hats As much of the body's heat is lost from the head, pack a woolly hat and

perhaps a peaked cap – but make sure that it has a string to attach to your jacket or the first good gust may whisk it away.

Sunglasses The reflection from the water will add to the sun's glare so these are a good idea – but make sure they have a retaining string attached; countless pairs of glasses must by now be littering the seabed. This advice applies to prescription glasses too.

Scarves A towelling scarf will help to stop water running down your neck.

Thin layers of lightweight clothing are better than thick jumpers.

Boarding

If the boat is moored alongside a pontoon you will probably have to step over the guardrails to get on board. When you do so don't use the guardrails or their supporting stanchions to hold on to, instead grab the steel shrouds that support the mast – they will be strong enough to bear your weight.

Other essentials

Don't forget to take any essential medicines and a few sticking plasters. If you think you are likely to be seasick, take some anti-seasickness tablets. Pack the usual bathroom items if you are away for a few days but keep them to the minimum as you won't have much locker space. Don't forget a small towel and lots of spare socks. Ask your skipper for advice on what else you may need: passport? Euros?

Skipper's briefing

Once you have been welcomed on board, stowed your gear and had a cup of coffee, your skipper will give everyone a safety briefing explaining:

♦ The layout of the boat
♦ Where fire-fighting equipment is kept and instructions on use
♦ Location and use of distress flares
♦ Use of lifejackets and safety harness (there should be one for every crew member)
♦ The operation of the liferaft
♦ The man overboard safety equipment; lifebuoys, danbuoys etc
♦ Location and use of the bilge pump
♦ The gas shut off valve

Your skipper will brief you on safety procedures and the boat's layout.

2 parts of the boat

Boatspeak

The diagram, opposite, shows how sections of the boat are named. These are essential to learn as they also relate to direction as well. Probably the most important are the terms *port* (left) and *starboard* (right); the front of the boat is the *bow* so if you see an object such as a marker buoy at the front right-hand side of the boat you tell the skipper that it is on the *starboard bow*.

If you are walking on deck towards the front of the boat or *bow*, you are going *forward* and when going to the *stern*, or back of the boat,

A very well-designed cockpit layout – all very neat and tidy.

you are going *aft*. When you want to go inside the boat down to the cabins, you say that you are going *below* and when you are coming up you are going *on deck*. To do that you usually have to pass through the *cockpit* which is an area lower than the deck where there will probably be seating.

Down below you will find a kitchen area known as the *galley*. The *forepeak* is the area right up in the bow. The toilet is called the *heads*.

The width of the boat is its *beam* so if you see a buoy beside the boat to your right, it is said to be *abeam to starboard*. *Ahead* is the area in front of the boat and *astern* behind the boat.

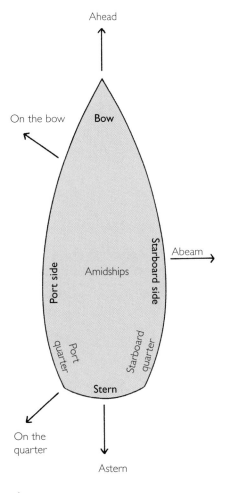

▲ *Directions from the boat.*

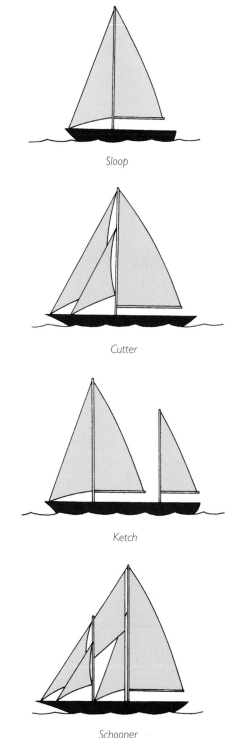

Types of rig

As you have probably already noticed, sailing boats come in many different shapes and sizes with different *rigs* – the term which describes the configuration of the masts and sails. The commonest cruising rig (the type of boat you are likely to be sailing on) is the *Bermudan sloop*

The mainsail on a gaff-rigged boat has four sides and is supported by a gaff – a pole or spar.

How the boat is rigged

Standing rigging

This term refers to the permanently fixed wire ropes that support the mast such as the *backstay* which can be tensioned to alter the bend of the mast.

The oddly named *shrouds* are wires that support the mast at the sides of the boat.

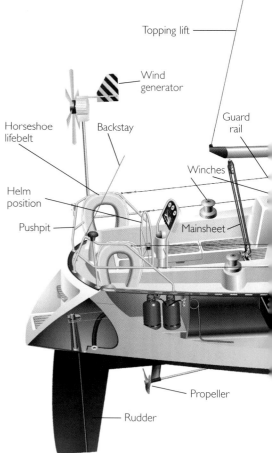

rig with one mast, with a mainsail and a separate headsail (see page 10). The *cutter* rig has one mast with a mainsail and two headsails. On larger sailing boats you may see two masts: the main and a smaller *mizzen* behind it. If the mizzen is forward of the rudder the boat is called a *ketch*; if it is positioned behind the steering gear the boat is known as a *yawl*. Generally the area of the yawl's mizzen is smaller than that of the ketch. A *schooner* also has two masts but this time the smaller one is before the main mast as you can see in the diagram on page 7.

Also popular today are the classic *gaff-rigged cruisers*, often based on traditional fishing boat types such as the Cornish Crabber. This rig has a mainmast with a quadrilateral or four-sided mainsail, the upper part of which is supported by a pole known as a *gaff*. A gaff cutter will have a *bowsprit*, a pole or *spar* which extends out at the bow to which a foresail is rigged.

Running rigging

This refers to the moveable wire ropes that hoist, lower and generally control sails, for example the *halyard* which is attached to the head of the mainsail to hoist it.

The diagram below gives an idea of the main types of standing and running rigging. The *topping lift* is the wire that attaches to the top of the mast and supports the *boom*, the horizontal spar. *Sheet* is another term for a rope or line and the *mainsheet* is the rope that that controls the mainsail. The *kicking strap*, sometimes known as the *vang* is attached to the boom to keep it from lifting.

The diagram also shows the names of parts on the body or *hull* of the boat. The *stanchions* support the guard rails, which are safety rails to prevent crew from falling overboard. The *pulpit* is a stainless steel frame at the bow to which the guardrails are attached; the *pushpit* is a similar frame at the stern.

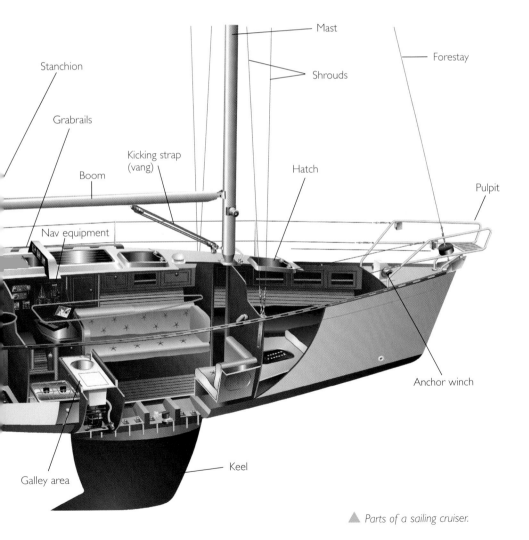

▲ *Parts of a sailing cruiser.*

Sails

The Bermudan rig has two basic sails: the *mainsail* which is secured vertically to the mast and horizontally to a pole called the *boom*. and the *headsail* a smaller triangular sail attached to the forestay.

The sails have a language of their own: the leading edge of the sail is the *luff* while the trailing edge is the lee-edge or *leech*. The top of the sail is the *head* and the bottom is the *foot*.

The *clew* is the lower rear corner of the sail, usually reinforced to take the *clew outhaul*, the line which tensions the *foot* of the sail. In the

Headsails

Jib This what the headsail will probably be called on your boat.

Foresail Another term for a headsail but used to refer to the lowest headsail on a square-rigger.

Genoa Usually a fairly large headsail which overlaps the mast, used in light to fresh winds.

Storm jib A very small jib made of heavy cloth which can be set in strong winds.

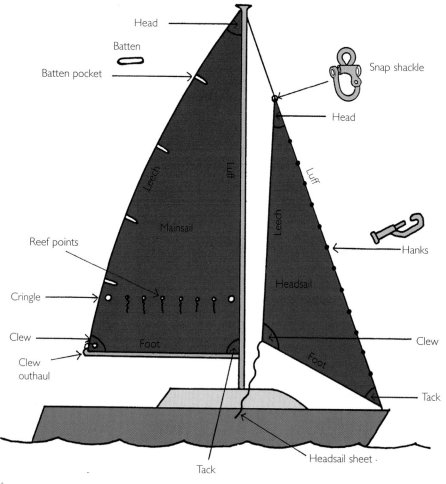

▲ *Parts of the sail.*

case of the headsail, the clew takes the headsail sheet which controls the sail.

Cringles are metal eyes set into the sail through which a rope can be passed.

Sometimes if the wind becomes very strong the mainsail will need to be reduced in size or *reefed*; there are reefing points on the sail for slab reefing (see page 38).

Battens are thin flexible plastic strips which are used to stiffen the leech of the sail.

The *tack* is the lower forward corner of a sail, not to be confused with the tack you do when you change course (see page 32–3).

3 knots & ropework

Everyone knows that sailors need to be able to tie good knots but don't worry, it is fun learning and you can impress your friends with a new skill and you will find some of the basic knots useful at home too.

Types of rope

Rope falls into three basic categories: *laid*, *plaited* and *braided*. Their construction is fairly self-explanatory but the fibres from which they are made are nowadays quite complex.

Natural fibres

In the past rope was made from natural materials such as hemp and sisal. These materials have largely been replaced by tougher synthetics but classic boats are often still rigged with traditionally-made rope.

Nylon

This is the strongest type of man-made fibre. It stretches and so has good shock-absorbing qualities, making it ideal for an anchor rope or *warp* or a mooring line.

Polyester

A material which is almost as strong as nylon but has less stretch in it, making it useful for sheets and halyards; it is available in pre-stretched form.

Polypropylene

Although this is not as strong as nylon or polyester, it is buoyant so is useful for floating lines such as those used for mooring a dinghy (the *painter*) or for the lifebuoy.

| *Left: Laid rope.* | *Centre: Braided rope (left) and plaited rope.* | *Right: Polypropylene.* |

Care of synthetic ropes

- Wash regularly to remove grit which can work its way into the fibres of the rope and cause damage.
- Leave to dry naturally; excessive heat will weaken the rope.
- Keep away from corrosive chemicals.
- Protect from chafe. Mooring lines should be protected by a section of plastic pipe or bound with cloth at the point where they go through a *fairlead* (fitting through which a working line passes eg on the bow to feed a mooring line through).

▼ *Parts of the rope.*

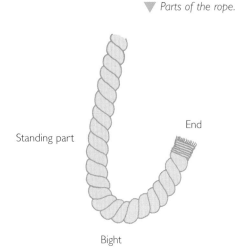

Standing part

End

Bight

One of the first lessons a new crewmember will learn is how to tie some basic knots.

Knots

One of the myths that most people have heard about sailing is that you have to be able to tie lots of complicated knots. This is not the case; yes you do need to be able to tie some basic knots, especially for mooring, but with a bit of practice you will find them easy. In fact you may enjoy knotting so much that you will want to increase your knowledge and skill – it can be a complete art-form.

Figure of eight
This is one of the simplest knots which is used as a stopper knot at the end of a sheet to stop it running right through a fitting.

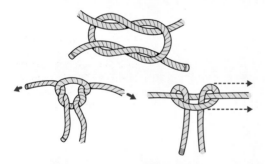

Reef knot
What every scout or guide learns to tie. It isn't a very secure knot, used mostly for tying in a reef on the mainsail.

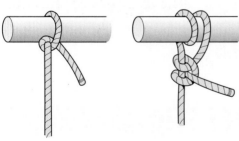

Round turn and two half hitches
A secure knot, but easy to undo; it is used for tying fenders to the boat or a line to a post or ring.

Bowline

Pronounced 'bo-lin'. The classic knot for making a secure standing loop to go over a mooring bollard. Quick to tie, it is also easy to release.

Fisherman's bend

Often used for 'bending' on the warp to the ring on an anchor. It is similar to a round turn and two half hitches but is more secure and holds well on a slippery rope.

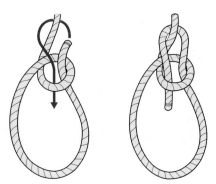

Sheet bend

A knot for tying two ropes together. The rope can be passed through twice to make a more secure double sheet bend (right).

Rolling hitch

This is used for fastening a rope to a spar, a chain or thicker rope to temporarily take the tension off. The direction of pull is across the final hitch and along the rope or spar.

Some knot terms

Bend Knot used to join two ropes

Bitter end The end of a rope

Bight A loop in a rope

Standing part The main part of a line

Hitch Loops which jam together well when under strain but which come apart easily when the strain is removed

Whipping A way of finishing off a rope end

Splicing A way of making a permanent eye in the rope, finishing the end of a rope or joining two ropes together

Winching

Winches are used to help crew to haul on a rope. A halyard (which hoists a sail) or sheet (a rope which controls a sail) is turned around a winch drum to take the strain when you are hoisting or sheeting in a sail. Haul the rope hand-over-hand, *never wrap the rope round your hand.*

The most important thing to remember when winching is to *keep your fingers well clear of the drum when there is strain on the rope.* The correct way to winch in is shown in the photo below (left) where you grip the rope firmly with

your fists clenched and kept well away from the drum. Don't hold the rope with your palm uppermost or your fingers will be trapped and injured (see photo below right). Some tension needs to be kept on the rope coming off the drum ('tailing'); another crew member will probably help you with this.

Many boats now have self-tailing winches which have a groove where you can jam the rope to keep the tension on the tail.

As the load becomes greater, extra power is applied with the winch handle. When the sail is correctly trimmed you then secure the rope to a cleat (see diagram below):

1 Start with a turn round the cleat.
2 Carry on with two or three cross turns.
3 Finish with a round turn to jam the rope.

If the cleat is self-jamming you will only need to

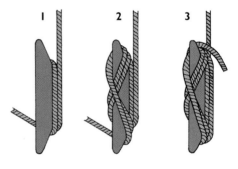

Turning a sheet around a winch drum.
Correct – the fists are clenched around the sheet and kept well away from the winch drum. ▼

Wrong – the fingers will be trapped against the winch drum. ▼

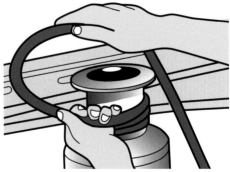

Winching: this crew is using the winch handle to add power – there is another crew behind him 'tailing' or keeping tension on the free end of the sheet.
Photo: www.stephenrichards.co.uk

A self-tailing winch makes it easier for one person to winch – the free end is jammed into the groove at the top of the winch to provide the necessary tension.

turn the rope once round the cleat to secure it. These will often be used for sheets as a self-jamming cleat enables the sheet to be released quickly.

After cleating a halyard, the remainder is coiled, starting from the end nearest to the cleat. About a third of a metre should be left between the cleat and the coil to make a bight or loop in the rope. This is twisted, passed through the coil and looped over the cleat.

Riding turns on a winch

Sometimes one turn on the winch drum slips over another and becomes jammed (see photo below); this is called a riding turn. It may happen when there are too many turns of rope on the winch drum or because the lead on or off the drum is incorrect.

A riding turn will usually free itself but if it becomes solidly jammed you can free it by attaching a line to the sheet using a rolling hitch (see page 15) to take off the tension. Once the load is off the sheet you can relay the turn on the drum.

Releasing a sheet

When you are asked to ease out a sheet, you put the flat palm of your hand against the turns on the winch drum. You hold the sheet in your other hand and gradually ease it out.

To fully release a sheet, lift it above the winch and pull the turns off the top.

Neatly coiled and secured rope is a sign of good seamanship.

Heaving a line

When you need to throw (*heave*) a line to some-one ashore for mooring there is a certain tech-nique to learn:

1 Coil the line carefully with no twists (the secret of success with this) and divide it into two, holding a half in each hand.

2 Swing the free-end half of the coil backward and forward to build momentum then throw. Allow the other half of the coil to run free.

Throwing a line needs a bit of practice so try and have a go before you to actually need do it so you can get the feel of it.

Coiling rope

Ropes have to be coiled neatly before being stowed or when you are about to moor. The diagram below shows you the stages of coiling a cable-laid rope:

1 Hold the rope in your left hand and coil in a clockwise direction. Twist the rope with your right hand as you pass each coil to your left hand; this stops the rope twisting.

2 When you have nearly finished coiling, bind the remaining rope end around the coils several times and pass a loop through the coils.

3 Bring the loop back over the top of the coils and push it downwards towards the loops binding the coils together. Pull the end tight to secure.

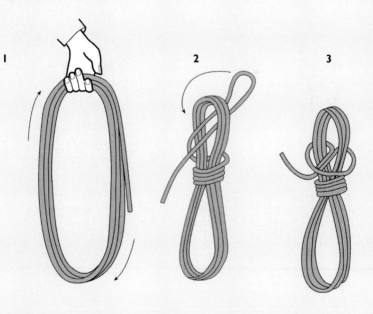

4 getting ready to sail

So you have all your gear stowed; the skipper has given everyone the safety briefing and told you the location of all the important items from the bilge pumps, flares and lifejackets to the tea and coffee in the galley. Now you can start to prepare the boat for going to sea.

Checklist for preparing the boat

* Crew safety briefing carried out
* All safety and firefighting equipment checked and ready for use
* All gear both above and below decks should be securely stowed
* Locker doors all secured
* The engine is checked and ready for starting with all cooling water stopcocks open
* Battery switch on
* Seacocks on toilets and sinks in sea-going position
* All hatches secured
* Water tanks full
* Fuel tanks full
* Gas bottles and gas taps turned off; spare full gas bottle available
* Bilge pumps checked
* Anchor secure and end of chain or warp made fast inboard
* Electronic nav equipment and radios checked
* Passage plan done and charts and plotting notes ready
* Weather forecast obtained
* Nav lights and torches checked if night sailing is planned
* Sail covers removed
* Mooring lines ready for slipping
* Burgee and ensign hoisted

Starting the engine

Your skipper will use the engine to get the boat clear of her berth and into open water.

Before the engine is started, the gear lever is put into neutral, the throttle is opened and the cooling water seacock is checked to make sure it is open.

Most engines are started with an ignition switch and a starter button. As soon as the engine is running, make sure that cooling water is circulating (usually by looking at the cooling water outlet). Diesel engines can be used as soon as they are started and do not like to idle too long. Petrol engines perform better when they have warmed up a bit.

TIP

To stop a petrol engine, you just turn off the ignition. A diesel engine usually has a separate stop lever which must be reset before the engine is used again.

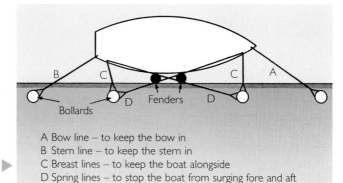

A Bow line – to keep the bow in
B Stern line – to keep the stern in
C Breast lines – to keep the boat alongside
D Spring lines – to stop the boat from surging fore and aft

The boat is secured with several lines. Fenders protect the boat from damage alongside. ▶

Casting off

If you are on a mooring then you just have one bow slip line to deal with (See Chapter 12) but it is more likely that you will join the boat on a pontoon berth in a marina or alongside a quay.

Unless a tidal stream is running, or a strong wind is blowing, leaving a pontoon or quayside is fairly straightforward. The boat will be secured by several lines as shown above. All the lines except the *breast lines* are removed, coiled and stowed. The breast lines are doubled back around a cleat or a bollard on shore so that they can easily be released from on board – these are then known as *slip lines*.

If there is a tidal stream running, one of the spring lines is left on to stop the boat moving backwards or forwards, depending on the direction of the tide. This spring can also be doubled back to act as a slip line. You may now be asked to stand by on deck with a spare fender (usually an inflated sausage), to protect the boat from possible damage to her sides.

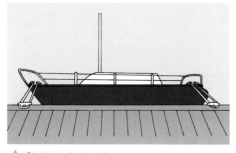

▲ *Slip lines doubled back around cleats.*

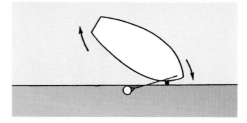

▲ *Fender positioned between bow and pontoon. Under power the boat pivots and the stern moves out.*

It may be necessary to move the stern of the boat away from the pontoon . This is done by slowly motoring forward against a spring line which has been passed around a bollard ashore. One end of the line is secured on board to a bow cleat; you may be asked to hold the other end while the skipper motors forward so that the boat pivots, taking the stern away from the pontoon. A fender is needed to protect the bow from the pontoon. Be ready to release the line when instructed and retrieve the fender.

Stowing lines and fenders

Once the boat is clear of her berth you will be asked to coil all the warps or mooring lines and stow them away neatly; any loose ropes left lying about will be a hazard on deck. If a rope is allowed to trail overboard it could get wrapped round the propeller.

Fenders should all be retrieved and stowed safely; it is bad form to leave them dangling over the side when you are on the move.

Leaving a raft of boats

Sometimes your boat may be positioned in the middle of a raft of boats moored alongside each other. If there is no-one else about to help when you are leaving, you and the rest of the crew need to follow the correct sequence of removing and refastening lines. The procedure for leaving a raft is shown in the diagrams below – B is your boat; note the direction of the tidal stream. You need to unfasten sufficient lines to create a gap for your boat to leave, while at the same time making sure that the other boats are under control ; it is your responsibility to ensure that the remaining boats are secure. It is very important that you know the purpose of each line and you know what you are doing – if in doubt, ask. You may need to stay with the outer boat until your skipper can manoeuvre into position to pick you up.

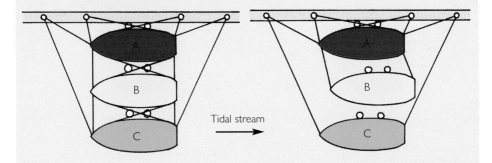

(**1**) Take off the bow and stern lines from your boat (B).

(**2**) Take off your spring and breast lines from C and the spring lines from A.

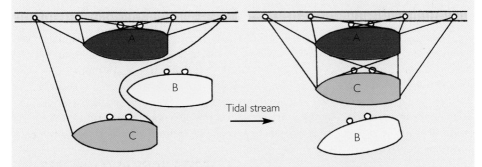

(**3**) Unfasten the stern line from C and lead it around the bows of your boat (B) securing it ashore. Unfasten the breast lines from boat A and manoeuvre clear. Leave a crew member ashore to secure spring and breast lines between boats A and C and to adjust the bow and stern lines on boat C.

(**4**) Pick up crew from boat C.

Hoisting the sails

The next job is to hoist the sails (photo right); this is done whilst the boat is still in calm waters. The boat is motored slowly forward with its bow into the wind (*head to wind*) with all the controlling ropes (*sheets*) kept slack so that the wind doesn't fill the sails. You may be asked to keep a look-out for other boats and to warn the skipper if they get close.

Lookout

Generally the helmsman keeps a sharp eye on what is happening around him but it is not always easy for him to see round the sails, so everyone needs to help to be his eyes – and ears, especially near harbours.

Any sighting of an approaching boat should be reported; big ships may look a long way off but they are travelling faster than you and it is surprising how quickly distances can be closed.

You may think that 'power should give way to sail' but in reality a supertanker travelling at 15 knots with a stopping distance measured in miles should be avoided by small vulnerable yachts! Photo: www.stephenrichard.co.uk

Mainsail

First the main *halyard* or rope which hoists the sail, is unshackled from its harbour stowage position and checked to see that it is not twisted. This is then shackled to the head of the mainsail.

With the boat head-to-wind you then unfasten the sail ties or shock cord securing the sail to the boom. The kicking strap, which holds down the boom is eased off. Wait for the order 'Up main' or 'Hoist main' and heave on the halyard to hoist the sail, looking upwards to make sure that the sail is not getting caught on the *shrouds*, the wires which support the mast at the sides, or the *spreaders*, the metal struts which keep the shrouds spread apart. The main halyard will probably run internally down the inside of the mast, emerging at the bottom through a *sheave*, a grooved wheel.

When the load gets heavy, take a turn round the winch drum. (If you are not sure which way the winch drum rotates, spin it by hand first to check.) Continue to haul until the load gets heavy then take a couple of turns round the drum and engage the winch handle for the final hoist. Once the sail is fully hoisted, remove the winch handle. Take care that it doesn't slide overboard.

TIP

The sail is fully hoisted when the *luff*, the leading edge of the sail – next to the mast has become taut.

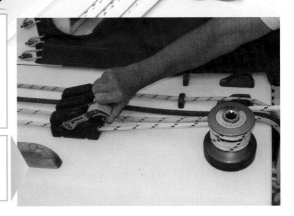

The mainsheet adjusts the sail and position of the boom. It runs through a system of blocks which attach to the boom and to a track on the deck called the traveller. This allows the sail to be adjusted by moving the position of the boom.

Jammers are types of cleat which tension and hold the sheets firmly. Like winches, care must be taken with these to avoid injury to fingers.

Preparing to heave on the halyard to hoist the mainsail.

The halyards need to be coiled and tidied away on the cleat under the winch. Then the *topping lift*, the line that supports the boom when the sails are down, is uncleated and eased off so that the *leech*, the trailing edge of the sail, takes the weight of the boom. Tighten the kicking strap and then pull in the *mainsheet*, which controls the sail, just enough to stabilise the boom and stop the sail *flogging*, (flapping) noisily.

Headsail

On many cruising boats the headsail is permanently hoisted on a roller and is self-furling. This means that the sail is wrapped round the forestay and unfurled or furled using lines round a winch or into a jamming cleat. This makes it very easy to use, especially if the sail needs to be reduced in size if the wind gets strong.

On your boat, however, the headsail or jib may be attached to the forestay with clips called hanks. You may be shown how to 'hank on' the jib (see photo and inset opposite).

Using the winch to hoist the mainsail.

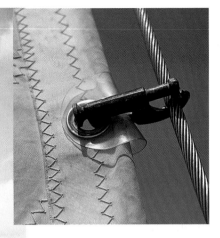

Hanking on the headsail. The luff of the sail is clipped on to a stay using a hank (see inset).

Deck log

As soon as the boat gets underway, the *deck log* (a written record of events on board), should be entered with the time of departure, and relevant details such as the set of the sails, engine running hours, wind direction and strength, speed and distance, course, barometric pressure etc. The navigator usually writes this up but you will probably be shown how to make entries.

Times are shown in four-figure notation using a 24-hour clock, for example 8.00am is written as 0800 and 8.00pm is 2000. Courses and bearings are given in three-figure notation through 360 degrees eg 290°.

When the jib needs to be hoisted, the boat doesn't need to point into the wind. First the halyard is secured to the head of the sail. The shock cord or sail ties are unfastened and the sheet is checked to make sure it is free to run. The halyard is turned round the headsail winch drum and then the sail is hoisted, using the winch handle if necessary. Once the sail is set, the halyard is cleated and the spare rope is coiled neatly.

When you have hoisted the headsail and secured it, lead the headsail sheet around the sheet winch drum (you will need two turns to start with) and haul it in, using the winch handle until it stops flapping. You may need to put an extra turn around the winch drum. Be careful not to trap your fingers. Also keep clear of the flapping headsail when it is being hoisted, especially if a shackle is fitted to the clew.

Once both sails have been hoisted, the boat can be set on course and the sheets adjusted. At this stage the engine will probably be stopped. Don't forget to tidy away winch handles and sail ties.

5 | how the boat sails

If you have sailed on a dinghy or tried windsurfing, the principles of how the boat uses the wind to sail will be familiar. However, if you have never sailed before, you may find the mechanics of boat handling a bit perplexing at first. But with practice, you will soon get the hang of it.

Is it a plane?

It is simple to grasp the principle that wind coming from behind the sails will push the boat along. But what if the wind is coming from a different direction? How do the sails work then?

The force of the wind can be harnessed so that the boat can sail in almost any direction except straight towards it. So how does this happen? Essentially the sail acts as an aerofoil in a similar way to an airplane wing: the speed of the airflow against the sail provides *lift* (see diagram). Lift can be simply explained as a combination of increased air pressure on the inner side of the sail and suction on the outer surface. A good way of demonstrating this is to run a tap and hold a spoon upside down with the water flowing over the bowl; you will notice that the spoon is sucked towards the flow. So the sail is pulled in the direction of the 'lift'; which can then be adjusted by altering the angle of the sail, known as *sail trim*.

OK, so if the driving force is coming across the beam then won't that make the boat go sideways? Probably – if the boat was flat-bottomed. But sailing boats have *centre boards* or *keels* on the bottom of the boat which helps to counteract the sideways motion or *drag*.

The principle of how a sail works is difficult to explain fully unless you enter the field of physics but the above will give you food for thought – once you are on the water as a crew member you can see for yourself how the airflow acts on the sails and the effects of sail trim.

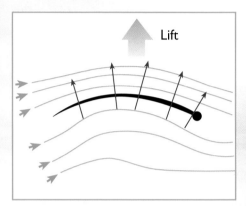

▲ As the wind passes round the wing-shaped sail the air flow on the leeward side speeds up and the pressure becomes lower than that on the windward side of the sail. This pressure difference creates a force as you can see in this diagram.

Steering

If you are asked to steer the boat using a *tiller* then the first thing you need to know is that you push it *away* from the direction that you want the bows of the boat to go! This is because the boat is steered by the force of the water acting against the rudder at the stern of the boat: the boat's stern is swung to *port* or *starboard* (left or right), causing the bows to move in the opposite direction.

If your boat has a wheel then the steering is configured so that you turn the wheel in the direction you want to go – just like driving a car.

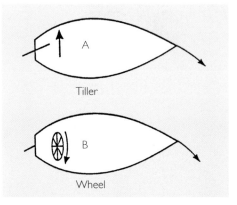

▲ *Steering by tiller or wheel.*

Sail trim

Your skipper will start to give instructions once you are under way about how the sails need to be trimmed or adjusted.

If you look at the diagram opposite you can get an idea of the relationship between the course and the angle of the sails relative to the direction that the wind is blowing from. You can see that the further the boat's bows are turned away from the wind, the more you need to ease out the sails. When the wind is blowing from directly behind the boat, the sails are fully out.

Points of sailing

The diagram opposite shows what is known as the points of sailing ie what angle and degree of sail trim you are likely to have in relation to the

> *Sailing upwind close-hauled on port tack – the crew is trimming the mainsail. Photo: www.stephenrichard.co.uk*

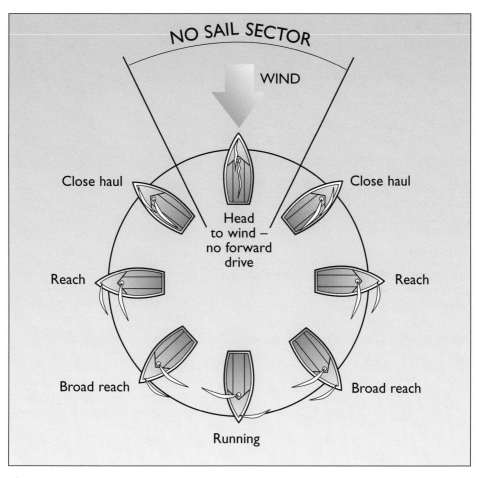

Points of sailing.

wind's position. You need to learn the terms which describe these points so when the skipper says that the boat is 'running', you know he means that the wind is directly behind you.

You cannot sail directly into the wind: there is a 'no sail sector' of about 90°. Some boats will

Knowing how much sail to take in comes with experience, but as a rough guide, you pull in the headsail until it stops flapping and then adjust the mainsail to the same angle.

sail closer to the wind than others but usually 45° is normal on each side.

When the boat is running before the wind, both sails may be on the same side; if the headsail is out to the opposite side to the mainsail, the sails are said to be *goosewinged*

Poling out the headsail

Sometimes a *whisker pole* may be attached by a hook to an eye on the mast and clipped onto the headsail sheet to hold the headsail out to windward when running goosewinged.

The pole is supported by an *uphaul*, a line attached to the mast and a *downhaul*, a line which stops it rising. A *guy line* may be attached to set the fore-and-aft position.

Sailing upwind

So you already know that you can't sail directly into the wind so what do you do if your course lies in that direction?

You have to sail in a zig-zag route either side of the wind's direction. This is called *beating to windward*. Each change of course is a *tack*. If the wind is on your starboard side and the boom is over the port side then you are on *starboard tack*. If the wind is on your port side and the boom is over the starboard side you are on *port tack*. So the tack is named opposite to the side where the boom lies. In racing, judging the time to change tack may make the difference in winning or losing; the aim is to point as high as possible. When cruising, the aim is to make good progress without tiring yourself out!

How to tack

In the diagram opposite, the boat is initially on starboard tack. To change tack or *go about*, the helmsman alerts the crew by saying 'ready about'. When the crew are ready he moves the tiller towards the sail which is the *leeward* side of the boat (the opposite way if wheel-steering) saying 'lee-oh'. This brings the boat's bows towards the wind. A crew member then lets go of the sheet holding the headsail on the port

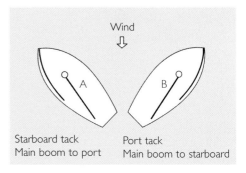

Wind

Starboard tack
Main boom to port

Port tack
Main boom to starboard

▲ *Starboard and port tacks.*

side and, as the bows move towards and through the wind, the sails flap and then fly across the boat to the other side. The crew then sheets in the headsail on the starboard side by turning the sheet round the starboard winch drum, using the winch handle if necessary, and cleats it in. The mainsail is then adjusted by the helmsman if he needs to – if you are staying *close hauled* (close to the wind), the mainsheet can normally be left cleated. You are now sailing on port tack.

> *Going about – changing from one tack to another by turning the bow through the wind.*

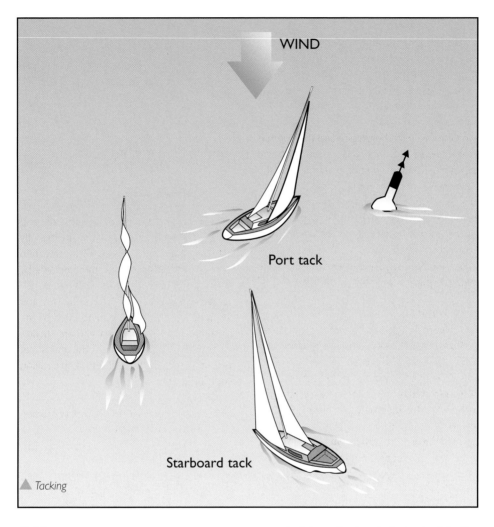

WIND

Port tack

Starboard tack

▲ *Tacking*

Gybing

The gybe can be regarded as the opposite to the tack as the boat is sailing with the wind astern so that stern of the boat passes through the wind not the bow. Unlike tacking, this action happens very suddenly so you need to be alert.

In the diagram (on page 34) your boat is on starboard tack and you are running before the wind towards a buoy. You want to go round the buoy so you need to gybe onto port tack.

As you approach the buoy, the helmsman shouts out 'stand by to gybe'. This alerts you to the fact that the boom is about to swing rapidly across so you need to keep clear. The crew pre-

pares to let go the headsail sheet while the helmsman hauls in the mainsheet fully to control the boom and stop it flying dangerously across the boat. He then says 'gybe-oh' and puts the tiller to *windward* (towards the sail) so that the stern travels through the wind. As the boom comes across and the wind fills the sail on the other side, he adjusts the helm and eases out the mainsheet. At the same time the crew member eases out the port headsail sheet and hauls in the starboard one, taking care not to let the headsail fly forward, as it may get twisted around the forestay.

The boat is now running on port tack, ready to alter course to round the buoy.

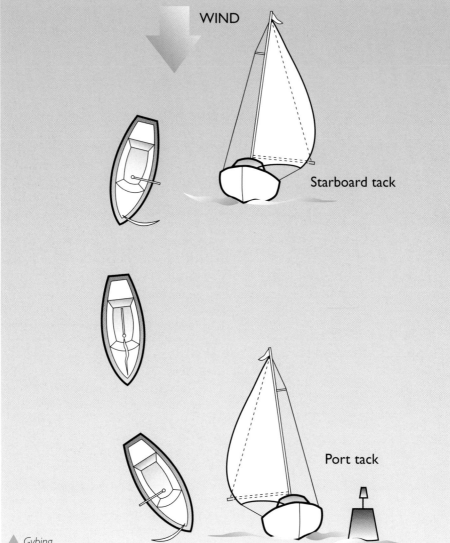

WIND

Starboard tack

Port tack

▲ Gybing

TIP

Preventer

To help to prevent an accidental gybe you can rig a line called a preventer. This is attached to the end of the main boom, led forward outside all the rigging, and passed through the bow fairlead back to the cockpit.

Some sailing terms to learn

Weather side or *windward* The side of the boat that is facing the wind.

Lee side or *leeward* The side of the boat away from the wind.

Heeling This is when the boat leans over to one side.

Luff up You may be told to 'luff up' when on the helm – this means to turn towards the wind.

Bear away This is when you turn away from the wind.

Beating or close-hauled

If you are beating, or sailing close-hauled, you are sailing close to the wind and the steering is influenced by the wind direction: too close and the sails will start to stall and the boat will lose speed; too far off the wind and you will also lose speed. This is probably the trickiest point of sailing and needs experience to get the best from the sails.

The helmsman tries to keep the boat sailing with the sails full (not flapping), allowing for any slight wind shifts. He assesses the mean direction he can steer and tells the navigator.

Reaching

This is probably the easiest point of sail for a beginner to helm because the angle of the wind isn't so critical and no longer dictates the course. It is also the fastest, so can be very exciting. The boat is *fine reaching* when the wind is forward of the beam; *reaching* when the wind is blowing directly on the side of the boat. *Broad reaching* is the point of sailing when the wind is on the aft quarter (near the back but not quite on the stern); the sails are eased out and the heeling angle of the boat decreases.

Running

When the wind is blowing on the stern of the boat the boat is said to be *running*. This may seem to be the easiest point of sailing as the sails are eased out and full but running can present problems. For a start, surprisingly, you won't be sailing as fast as when on a reach because turbulent air flow causes the sails to stall and lose lift. An answer to this is to use a *spinnaker*, a triangular sail that is 'flown' in front of the mast, set on a pole. These 'kites' as they are often called take some handling and are mostly used by racing crews. A spinnaker can increase the boat's tendency to roll – one of the problems experienced when running.

Another potentially serious problem when you are on a run is that of the accidental gybe when you have turned too far away from the wind and the booms slams across the boat. So when you first take the helm when on a run, make sure you have an experienced eye behind you.

These Cornish Shrimpers are running before the wind.

TIP

Telltales

You may have noticed some small lengths of nylon, cotton yarn or ribbon fixed on both sides of a sail. These are *telltales* which indicate to the helmsman the air flow over the sail. Racing sailors keenly watch their telltales (usually attached to the leech) which act as indicators for fine-tuning their sails for maximum performance. Broadly speaking, if the telltales are streaming aft on both sides of the sail, it is correctly sheeted. Experience at trimming the sails will tell you how to read these useful indicators.

Choppy weather

Although it may be fine and sunny with light winds when you set off, you always have to anticipate a change in the weather with stiffening breezes and a bit of a chop.

If the wind picks up quite a bit, the skipper will probably decide to reduce the mainsail area. This is done by *reefing* – the method of doing it varies from boat to boat but mostly it is done by either *slab reefing* or *roller reefing*.

In a blow, you have to make the decision to reef early and make sure that the sail area is reduced enough. Reefing is easier if the boat is hove-to which is when the boat is positioned into the wind with the mainsail to leeward and the headsail sheeted into windward. This effectively stops forward motion and steadies the boat; there will however be sideways movement due to leeway.

Lively seas

If the weather gets a bit brisk and you are experiencing a bit of blow, this can make very exciting sailing but you need to be prepared:

- All gear above deck should be secured and everything mobile below decks should be stowed safely as you don't want saucepans and coffee mugs flying around.
- Check that all hatches are secured and wash boards (to prevent water pouring into the cabin) are in place.
- If you think that the blow is likely to last then make up some hot drinks, sandwiches and get out some chocolate bars and other comfort snacks.
- Any crew members who are working on deck need to wear a lifejacket and safety harness and be clipped on.

Slab reefing

This method involves the sail being flaked down on the top of the boom (see diagram on page 40).

1 Ease the kicking strap and tension the topping lift to take the strain once the sail is released. Take the securing pin out of the mast so the sail luff can be freed.
2 Loosen the main halyard and slightly drop the sail.
3 Hook the luff cringle (eyelet) over the reefing horn and haul the leech cringle down to the boom with the reefing line. The luff cringle now becomes the tack of the reefed sail.
4 Hoist the sail, ease out the topping lift and adjust the kicking strap.
5 Secure the loose sail with a line threaded through small eyelets in the sail and round the boom.

Roller reefing

You may come across the form of roller reefing where the sail is wound round the boom. This can be a more controllable system than slab reefing but can be heavy work for the crew as it involves winding in the sail on a rotating boom (see diagram on page 40).

You can reduce a substantial amount of sail area but the sail will not set as well as when using slab reefing. But it can have the advantage of the controls being led into the cockpit.

Disadvantages are that you need to watch that the sail luff doesn't crease up and you can't roller reef a mainsail that has conventional stiffening battens. Here is how it is done:

1 Take off the kicking strap and tension the topping lift.
2 Take the pin out of the mast so that the luff can be freed up.

3 Uncleat the halyard and ease down the sail, turning the reefing handle at the same time.
4 The sail should be pulled tight at the leech to make it roll evenly. Care should be taken to prevent the luff fouling the reefing gear.
5 When the sail has been reduced sufficiently, remove or secure the reefing handle.
6 Hoist the sail, replace the securing pin, cleat the halyard and ease out the topping lift.

You won't be able to put the kicking strap back on again once the sail is reefed because the sail is wrapped round the boom but you could fit a reefing or boom claw (see insert in the diagram) over the boom.

A slab reef in the mainsail.
Photo: stephenrichard.co.uk

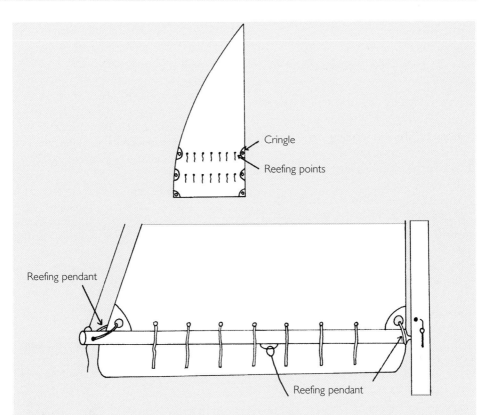

Cringle

Reefing points

Reefing pendant

Reefing pendant

Points reefing Ease the kicking strap and tension the topping lift. Take the securing pin out of the mast so that the luff of the sail can be pulled out of the mast track. Uncleat the main halyard and lower the mainsail to a position where the luff cringle can be lashed to the boom. Feed a short length of line (called a reefing pendant) through the luff cringle and lash it to the boom. The pendant for the leech cringle may be permanently attached to one side of the boom and all that is necessary is to pass it through the cringle and secure it to a block on the other side of the boom.

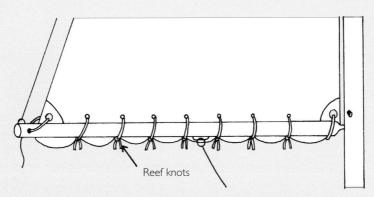

Reef knots

Hoist the sail, replace the securing pin in the mast, cleat the halyard, ease out the topping lift and tension the kicking strap. Roll up the loose sail and secure by tying together (under the boom) the reefing points from either side of the sail. Use reef knots for this. When taking the reef out, untie the reefing points before the reefing pendants or the sail may tear.

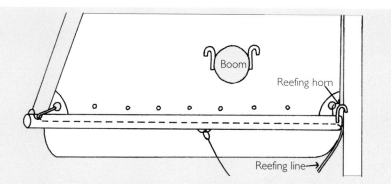

Slab reefing The luff cringle is hooked over the reefing horn and the leech cringle pulled down to the boom using the reefing line.

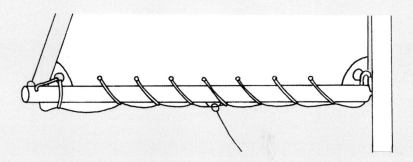

Roll up the loose sail and spiral a light line through the eyelets in the sail and around the boom, securing it at both ends. When taking the reef out, remove the light line first.

Roller reefing With this method any amount of sail can be reduced, but the sail does not set as well as when using the other methods. The kicking strap cannot be used because the sail is rolled around the boom. One solution is to fit a reefing claw over the rolled sail.

In-mast reefing

With this system the mainsail is wound on a roller inside the mast.

Reefing the headsail

Most sailing cruisers now have self-furling headsails where the sail is permanently hoisted and is reefed by rolling the sail round the forestay. The furling line is led round a drum sited at the bottom of the forestay and often into the cockpit. You ease out the sheet as you steadily haul on the furling line, keeping an even tension.

Headsail reefing. The furling line leading from the drum on the forestay.

Lee shore

It is very dangerous to sail close to a lee shore when a strong onshore wind is blowing. The boat can be blown onto it and damaged. So if you think that you are likely to be sailing close to a lee shore is safer to alter your course.

Sometimes your skipper may decide that if you are approaching an unsheltered harbour or anchorage with a stiff onshore wind blowing, then it is safer to either stay out at sea or head for a more sheltered destination.

This headsail is partially reefed. You can see the slab reefed mainsail behind the headsail.

6 finding the way

So you are now getting familiar with the boat and how she sails but how do you find out how to get from one harbour to another?

Instead of having maps, as on land, sailors have charts which show coastal features but also, importantly, depths of water and hazards such as fast tides and sandbanks, which could cause you to run aground at low tide if you don't know where they are. The chart will also show you all the navigational buoys and seamarks.

There are also pilot books published that give details on harbour approaches, anchorages, tidal conditions, local weather patterns and other useful information.

The theory of coastal navigation, which includes chart plotting, can be learned at evening classes during the winter. You will find it useful – and interesting – to know about pilotage which is navigation by using buoys, lighthouses, beacons, towers and other marks. You will learn to recognise these by day or night and to locate their positions on a chart.

Buoyage

The system of buoyage around north-west Europe has been developed by the International Association of Lighthouse Authorities (IALA) and is called System A. In North America System B is used.

▲ *The conventional direction of buoyage in the British Isles follows the arrows shown.*

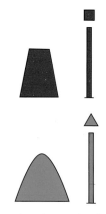

A green starboard hand beacon showing the outer limit of the safe channel coming into harbour.

Lateral marks

A lateral mark shows the port or starboard side of a channel as it relates to the Conventional Direction of Buoyage. This is shown by a broad arrow on large-scale charts – usually in a clockwise direction round land masses or in the general direction of approach from seaward when entering a harbour, estuary or river.

When you are making an approach to harbour, you leave the red cylindrical-shaped buoys or marks to your *port* (left) and the green conical buoys to *starboard* (right). Their shapes may vary (see diagrams right).

It is essential to stay between these buoys as they indicate the safe channel to follow. Where the channel divides, the lateral marks are modified by a green or red horizontal band which indicates the main or preferred channel.

▲ *Lateral marks: port hand (above) and starboard (below).*

Red port hand lateral buoy.

Green conical starboard buoy.

Cardinal marks

These are pillar-shaped buoys with black and yellow horizontal bands and black top marks. They are placed north, south, east and west of known dangers. You need to memorise the topmarks to identify where it is safe to sail:

North – this is easy as it has arrows pointing upwards.
South – no problem here as the arrows point downwards.
East – Two arrows point up and down rather like an **E**aster Egg!
West – Two arrows point to each other – like a **W**ine glass shape.

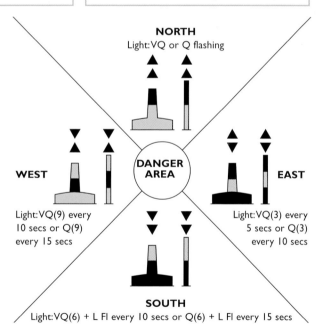

NORTH
Light: VQ or Q flashing

WEST
Light: VQ(9) every 10 secs or Q(9) every 15 secs

DANGER AREA

EAST
Light: VQ(3) every 5 secs or Q(3) every 10 secs

SOUTH
Light: VQ(6) + L Fl every 10 secs or Q(6) + L Fl every 15 secs

TIP

If you can't see the topmark clearly then the placing of the bands will help you to identify the buoy as the black band corresponds to the way the topmark points. At night cardinal buoys have flashing lights which will tell you the buoy's position; the flashes correspond to a clock face. For example, the north cardinal (12 o'clock) will flash continuously; east will flash in groups of 3, south flashes in groups of 6 and west in groups of 9.

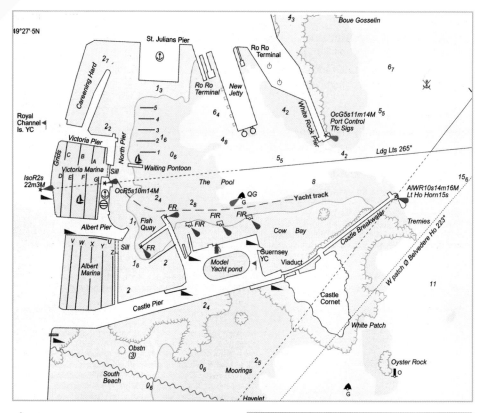

On this Reeds Nautical Almanac *chart extract you can see representations of green and red channel markers, cardinal buoys and lights.*

As you sail up river you may see tree branches, known as withies, stuck into the mud to mark the edge of the channel.

Isolated danger marks

A known danger such as wreck or a clump of rocks which is surrounded by deep water is usually directly marked with an *isolated danger mark*. The buoy has black and red horizontal bands and carries two large black round top-marks. It may have a white light which flashes in groups of two.

Safe water marks

These red and white vertically-striped buoys indicate that there is safe, navigable water all round them. They are used as landfall or mid-channel marks.

Special marks

You may see the odd yellow buoy as you are sailing. These are *special marks* and denote areas and features such as traffic separation schemes, military firing grounds, water skiing and bathing areas, outfall pipes and cables.

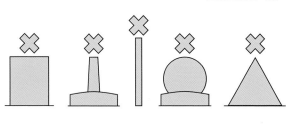

Light – Alt. Blue/Yellow

▲ This is a temporary buoy used as an emergency marker following a wreckage.

Safe water buoy.

Shore lights and transits

On or near the land there are also fixed seamarks such as lighthouses and lit beacons which you can use to determine your position by day or night. In the dark the lights each have specific characteristics (see page 49), which are marked on the chart, to enable you to identify them.

Two shore objects, which can be things like water towers, churches or conspicuous buildings, are often used to navigate safe entry to a harbour or river. Such marks are called leading marks or transits.

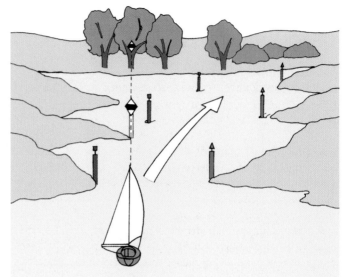

▲ *A transit. The boat lines up the diamonds to enter the river and then keeps between the port and starboard marks.*

Sectored lights

These are very useful when entering harbour at night. The light marking a safe channel (probably from a lighthouse or beacon) can only be seen when approached from a certain angle. In the example given right you can see that provided that you stay in the white sector shown by light A you avoid dangerous rocks. Then when you see the white sector from light B, it is safe to turn to port. So if you can see the green or red lights from either light then you know you are off course.

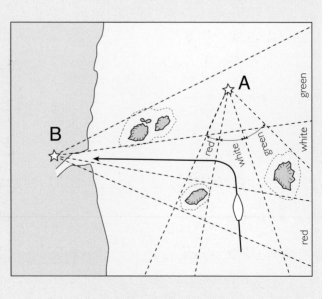

Channel marks

Approaches to ports and harbours from rivers and estuaries are marked with preferred channel buoys which are coloured red and green.

Light characteristics

Lights on buoys, lighthouses and beacons work on regular cycles, displaying specific characteristics which identify them (marked on charts).

Below are examples of the types of light you are likely to see at night. The time in seconds that a light takes to display its complete characteristic, which includes the time when it is not lit, is called the *period*.

It is a good idea to use a watch to time a light that you are trying to identify as it is easy to imagine that the light you are looking at is the one you are expecting unless you check very carefully.

The light characteristics for this west cardinal buoy are 9 very quick flashes every 10 seconds or 9 quick flashes every 15 seconds.

Fixed (F). A light which is on all the time.

![Flashing diagram]

Flashing (Fl). The dark period exceeds the light period.

![Quick Flashing diagram]

Quick Flashing (Q). 50–79 flashes per minute.

![Very Quick Flashing diagram]

Very Quick Flashing (VQ). 80–159 flashes per minute.

![Ultra Quick Flashing diagram]

Ultra Quick Flashing (UQ). 160 or more flashes per minute.

![Long Flashing diagram]

Long Flashing (LFl). Flash 2 seconds or longer.

Group Flashing (Fl). A number of flashes within a certain time period: Fl(3).

![Occulting diagram]

Occulting (Oc). The light period exceeds the dark period.

Group Occulting (Oc). A number of occults within a certain time period: Oc(3).

Isophase (Iso). The periods of light and dark are equal.

Morse (Mo(a)). Shows a morse letter (in this case 'A').

7 steering a course

When you are out of sight of land and there are no suitable marks, the compass is used to find the direction you want to go; this is known as steering a course.

Compasses

A compass points towards magnetic north – not to the North Pole.

It has magnetic needles which are horizontally mounted, free to swing in the direction of north. There will also be a lubber line which is a fixed line showing the fore-and-aft line of the boat.

The electronic compass

An electromagnetic compass (right) uses an electronic sensor to detect the Earth's magnetic field and display a heading in digital form. It can also be linked to other onboard equipment.

The DataScope hand bearing electronic compass is a very handy piece of kit which combines a digital compass, an electronic rangefinder and a chronometer in a handheld unit. It computes range and bearing and stores nine separate bearings together with the times they were taken.

How do you use a compass?

You line up the course you want with the lubber line or, in the case of an electronic compass, the digital display and steer the boat to keep on course.

Steering an accurate course is a bit tricky to begin with: when you look at the compass, the card appears to swing when in fact it is the boat that is swinging around. It is better to practise when the sea is calm or you are moving under power.

To orientate yourself, try moving the helm slightly and see which way the figures on the

The boat's main compass has to be carefully sited to avoid its accuracy being affected by metal items.

display appear to move; move the helm back into the original position to regain the course. Don't forget to look up frequently to keep aware of what is around you.

Influences on the compass

The Earth is like a big magnet with two magnetic Poles: north and south; magnetic *meridians* are lines of force pointing to the Poles.

The magnetic Poles don't coincide with the true geographical Poles. The angle between a magnetic meridian and a geographical or *true* meridian is called *variation* (see diagram).

Variation

Variation can be either west or east and when applied to a charted course it then becomes a *magnetic course* which is shown by the letter M after the figures eg 148° M. When you correct a true course to magnetic, westerly variation is added and easterly variation is subtracted; here is an example:

True course	142° T +
Variation 6° west	6°
Magnetic course	148° M

If you look at a nautical chart you find a compass shaped drawing called a compass rose. This gives the variation as calculated when the chart was last updated plus the number of *minutes* (the scale on the chart is measured in degrees, subdivided into *minutes* – there are 60 minutes in a degree) that represent the annual change.

Deviation

The compass can be affected by ferrous metal, electrical and electronic systems and anything that may contain a magnet. This means that you have to make sure that the main boat's compass is sited well away from anything which may cause compass *deviation*.

Deviation alters with different boat headings so a table is needed to show how to correct the compass.

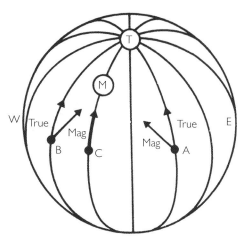

▲ *Variation. Magnetic north M is offset slightly from true north T, so the variation between the two will depend on where you are on the Earth's surface in relation to them. At point B variation is east, at A it is west, whilst at C the variation is nil since true and magnetic north are directly in line.*

One way a skipper can make his own deviation table is take a series of compass bearings using known landmarks. When two marks can be seen in line from the boat they are said to be *in transit*. If the boat is sailed across this transit on various headings the deviation can be noted for each heading.

Once you know the deviation figure you add westerly and subtract easterly deviation to the magnetic course to get a *compass course* to steer. A compass course is shown by the letter C eg 143° C.

Watch out for metal items left lying around such as cans, penknives, tools as these will affect the compass.

Taking bearings

If you want to find the direction of a landmark on the shoreline from the boat, you use a *hand-bearing compass*. This direction from the object is known as a bearing. You don't have to worry about deviation, provided that you are not standing next to the main compass or any other magnetic or metal influences. You still need to take account of variation.

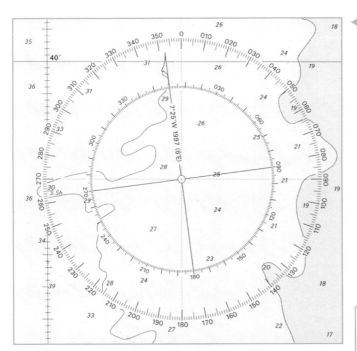

Compass rose.

Taking a bearing using a hand-bearing compass.

To take a bearing, hold the compass steady and align the V sight with the landmark. When the card stops swinging, make a note of the figure under the line on the compass or under the V sight. This is the magnetic bearing of the land-mark from the boat.

The photo (right) shows a mini hand-bearing compass which is being held at eye level. The landmark is sighted over the edge of the compass and you take a reading from the prism below.

It is hard to get an accurate bearing on a pitching or rolling boat as the the compass is sensitive to movement. So if the weather is rough you will need to take several readings. Note the time the bearings were taken.

8 how to read a chart

What is a chart?

A chart is a sailor's map of the sea. It is used to identify the boat's position and destination – and the best route between the two.

Latitude and longitude

In the diagram below you can see the Earth overlaid with imaginary lines that converge at the poles called *meridians of longitude*. The meridian passing through Greenwich is the datum meridian for longitude It is 0°, increasing to 180° east and west of the Greenwich meridian.

The diagram below shows *parallels of latitude* and, unlike the meridians of longitude, are more or less equally spaced, but they do very gradually get further apart the further they are from the Equator.

Latitude and longitude are always used together to define a position which are measured in degrees (°) which are subdivided into minutes (′). There are 60 minutes in one degree. Sixty degrees, ten point five minutes would be written: 60° 10′.5

Nautical miles

As the meridians of longitude converge towards the poles, they are no good for measuring distance. Instead we use the parallels of latitude for distance as they remain more or less equidistant from each other. But because, as we saw above, they gradually increase you need to use the latitude scale level which your boat's position.

One minute of latitude represents one nautical mile (6076ft/1852m) which is a bit longer than a land mile which is 5280ft.

How do we make the Earth flat?

To be able to plot our way, we need to project the curved Earth out on a chart. The main type of projection you will come across for coastal sailing is called Mercator.

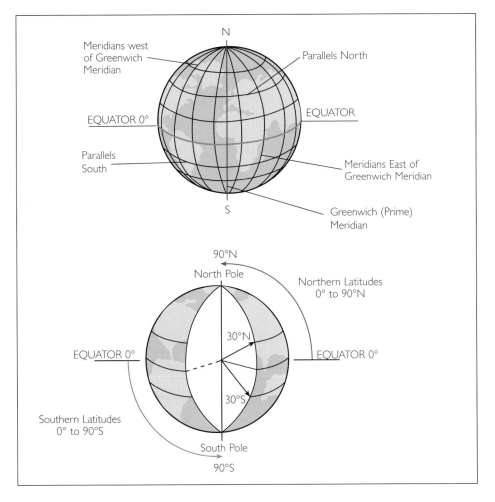

What is on the chart?

When you study a chart you will see lots of fascinating symbols and abbreviations for buoyage, depths, anchorages and dangers. These are all listed in an Admiralty publication: *Chart 5011*. But the diagram shown here gives you a few examples

~~~~~ Overfalls, tide rips, races

Eddies

Obstn   Obstn   Obstruction or danger, exact nature not specified or determined, depth unknown

(4₆)   Obstn   Obstruction, depth known

(4₆)   Obstn   Obstruction which has been swept by wire to the depth shown

(5₈) 19   18 Br   Breakers

(3·1)   (1·7)   (·4·1)   Rock which does not cover, height above high water

(1₆) (1₆) (5₈)   Rock which covers and uncovers, height above chart datum

Rock awash at the level of chart datum

Underwater rock, depth unknown, considered dangerous to surface navigation

Wk   Wreck showing any part of hull or superstructure at the level of chart datum

Wreck, depth unknown which is considered dangerous to surface navigation

Mast (1·2) Funnel Mast(1₂)   Masts   Wreck of which the mast(s) only are visible at chart datum

▲ *A complete list of symbols and abbreviations is provided in the Admiralty publication, Chart 5011.*

Rocks

Chart symbols for dangerous rocks are shown here together with a profile which gives you an idea of how they would look underwater.

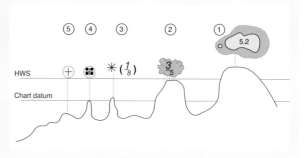

1 Rock which does not cover. The figure shown is the height above mean high water springs (MHWS).

2 This indicates a rock which covers and uncovers. The height above chart datum is given if known. The underlined figure indicates the drying height ie the rock is 3.5 metres above the level of chart datum.

3 A star (which could have a dotted circle round it) shows a small rock which, like 2, covers and uncovers.

4 A cross with dots in its angles shows a rock which is awash at chart datum level.

5 A cross without dots shows a rock of which the depth is unknown but could be a danger.

Who publishes charts?

The United Kingdom Hydrographic Office publishes Admiralty charts with worldwide coverage.

They also publish Admiralty Leisure Folios which consist of sets of charts for areas frequently used by yachtsmen. Admiralty charts are available from registered chart agents – usually chandlers.

Imray Laurie Norie and Wilson produce a series of charts for yachtsmen for UK waters and northwest Europe.

Stanfords publish charts for northwest Europe. Harbour charts are available for some areas consisting of several chartlets of harbours and stretches of intervening coastline.

Chart corrections

For charts to be reliable, they must be regularly corrected to include additional or changed navigational information.

Corrections to Admiralty charts can by made by returning the chart to the chart agent or by applying the corrections found in *Admiralty Notices to Mariners*, Weekly Edition. For more information go to www.ukho.gov.uk or for online updates for Admiralty Leisure Folios go to www.admiraltyleisure.co.uk.

Nautical publications

The Admiralty also publish a wide range of guides to symbols, tides, radio signals and lights and fog signals. They also produce *Sailing Directions NP1-72* which give details of land features, off-lying dangers, tidal streams, buoyage systems, port entrances and channels.

Various companies publish nautical almanacs such as *Reeds Nautical Almanac*. This gives port information, harbour charts, times and heights of tides, tidal stream diagrams, radio services, lists of lights and many other details.

There are also a variety of books giving sailing directions, known as pilot books which are invaluable to small boat users. They are frequently written from the sailor's point of view and are compiled and updated from information supplied by readers.

9 weather watching

When you are at sea, the state of the weather is obviously a subject that is of huge importance to you, as a sailor. Not only does it affect your enjoyment of the day's sailing but it also affects your safety too.

You need to be able to read the signs, as well as to understand the weather report, so personal observation is very important.

Weather lore

Red sky at night sailors' delight
Red sky in the morning sailors' warning

These old sayings – are they really relevant? Well there is certainly some truth in them. In the evening the red sky is thought to be caused by light reflecting off dust particles trapped by high pressure from the west, so it is a sign of good weather to come. In the morning the red sky is probably caused by the light reflecting off water vapour or ice crystals in very high wispy cirrus clouds which indicate a weather front approaching and the probability of rain later in the day.

Clouds

Cirrus clouds look like pretty wisps or threads across the sky; they are often called 'mares tails' because they look like horses' tails. They are very high clouds made of ice crystals and, can be a sign of a weather front approaching.

Cirrostratus clouds form a thin veil-like layer; they are also made up of ice crystals and are a sign that rain is on its way.

Cumulus clouds are the familiar fluffy cotton balls – if they stay small then fine weather is probably going to continue but if they start to grow and develop towers and turrets with flat bases, watch out for showers. If the cumulus clouds grow even bigger with flat anvil-like tops then you are in for squally rain and even thunderstorms.

Cirrocumulus and cirrus clouds form the distinctive 'mackerel sky' which may be the sign of a slow-moving weather front.

Fine sailing – small cumulus with a hint of cirrocumulus (mackerel sky) top right.

Growing banks of cumulus clouds are an indication of a cold front approaching. These seem to be developing into cumulonimbus which may bring squalls.

A glorious sunset like this will hopefully bring you a fine sailing morning.

Winds

One of your chief areas of weather interest will, of course be the wind. The basic explanation of winds is quite simple: hot air rises and creates low pressure on the Earth's surface while cold air falls and causes high pressure. Air tends to flow from high pressure to low pressure creating winds.

Sir Francis Beaufort, a British naval officer devised a way for sailors to estimate the wind by using visual signs – out at sea you look at how the waves behave and wind speed, wave height and appearance are listed on the Beaufort scale wind forces up to 8 are given below.

Beaufort Wind Scale

No	Description	Limit of mean wind speed knots	Appearance	Approximate wave height (metres)
0	Calm	Less than 1	Sea like a mirror.	0
1	Light airs	1 to 3	Ripples like scales.	Less than 0.1
2	Light breeze	4 to 6	Small wavelets. Glassy crests which do not break	0.1 to 0.3
3	Gentle breeze	7 to 10	Large wavelets. A few white horses.	0.3 to 0.9
4	Moderate breeze	11 to 16	Longer small waves. Frequent white horses.	0.9 to 1.5
5	Fresh breeze	17 to 21	Moderate waves. Many white horses.	1.5 to 2.5
6	Strong breeze	22 to 27	Large waves. White foam crests. Some spray.	2.5 to 4
7	Near gale	28 to 33	Sea heaps up. Waves break. Streaks of foam.	4 to 6
8	Gale	34 to 40	Moderately high, long waves. Crests break into spindrift. Extensive streaks of foam.	6 to 8

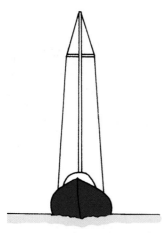

Beaufort force 0: The boat is motoring.

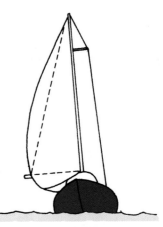

Beaufort force 3: The boat is sailing with a large genoa and full mainsail.

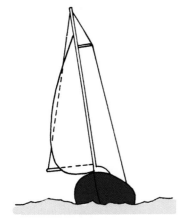

Beaufort force 5: The boat sails well with a jib and full mainsail.

Beaufort force 7: The boat sails with a storm jib and reefed mainsail.

Beaufort force 8: The boat runs with only a storm jib.

 ▲ *How the boat responds to different wind strengths.*

TIP

If you are caught out in a storm and everyone is tired and feeling sick, it is often best to heave-to. It can be dangerous to try to run for harbour.

Barometers

Many boats have a barometer on board to measure atmospheric pressure. A drop or rise in pressure can give you useful warnings about changes in the weather.

Barometric pressure ranges from about 960 millibars to 1040 millibars. High pressure indicates fine weather and low pressure is a sign of unsettled weather. Here are a few tips to reading the barometer:

Rising rapidly Initially better weather, but it may not last long.
Falling rapidly Bad weather on the way, possibly with gales.
Rising steadily A sign of good weather.
Falling steadily A sign of bad weather.

A masthead wind indicator will give you a fairly accurate reading of wind speed.

Weather forecasts

One of the most important tasks you need to do when planning to go to sea is a weather check. You will notice that there seem lots of different sources – but most of the weather forecasts given out in the UK originate from the Meteorological Office (www.metoffice.gov.uk).

There is a wide variety of ways of obtaining a Met office weather forecast, ranging from radio and television broadcasts, landline-based calls and faxes, to downloads onto mobile phones and computers.

Marinecall

The most relevant and useful service which you will probably use is Marinecall, accessed by phone, fax, mobile or internet subscription. It provides all kinds of weather reports for different sea areas from current weather conditions through to long-term assessments with synoptic charts. If you go onto the Met Office website and click onto Marinecall you will see how to get a free guide to their services and how to receive them.

Two-day forecasts are currently updated twice a day at 0700 and 1900; five-day forecasts are updated at 0700.

BBC shipping forecasts

These are broadcast daily on Radio Four on Long Wave (LW) with a frequency of 198kHz at 0048, 0520, 1201 and 1754 local time (weather forecasts are given using the 24 hour clock). Some transmissions are on VHF. If you have internet access the easiest way to pick them up is at www.bbc.co.uk/weather. Here is an example of the start of a typical shipping forecast:

> *And now the shipping forecast issued by the Met Office on behalf of the Maritime and Coastguard Agency at 0505 on Thursday 2 November.*
>
> *There are warnings of gales in German Bight, Biscay and Fitzroy. The general synopsis at midnight: high (pressure) Northern Ireland 1037 (barometric pressure) expected Irish Sea 1036 by midnight tonight. New low (pressure) expected Trafalgar 1010 by the same time.*

Inshore waters forecast

These are more detailed Met office forecasts also easily accessed through the BBC weather website and cover 31 areas listed from Cape

Wrath in the north of Scotland to the Isle of Man. An example of an inshore forecast:

Lyme Regis to Lands End including the Isles of Scilly issued by the Met Office at 0500 UTC on Thursday 2 November. 24 hour forecast: wind northerly veering easterly 4 (Beaufort scale) occasionally 5 in west. Weather fair; visibility good; sea state smooth or slight, locally moderate in the west later.

Coastal forecasts

For a very local forecast in your sailing area the coastal forecasts will give you lots of detail:

Weymouth and Lyme Bay (St Albans Head to Start Point) 2 November
1200–1800 (time)
Pressure: 1036 mB F; temp max/min: 10/3 degrees C
Wind speed: F3-4 (Beaufort scale) becoming F2-4, wind direction NE;
Maximum gusts in knots 18 becoming 20.
Visibility: very good becoming good.

Altogether it looks a good afternoon for a sail!

On the BBC website you can access UK Hydrographic Office tide tables for specific harbours complete with tidal graphs.

HM Coastguard

You can contact your local Coastguard station for a short and long-term weather forecast and advice on tide times for the area. Telephone numbers are given below (correct as of summer 2007).

The Coastguard also broadcasts Inshore Waters forecasts 4 hourly (updated twice daily) bulletins on marine MF and VHF channels. These broadcasts also include any gale or strong wind warnings. If winds are likely to reach force 6 and over, the warning is repeated every two hours.

Navtex

To get Navtex forecasts, your skipper needs a dedicated receiver on board. The service automatically broadcasts localised urgent maritime safety information on 518kHz which includes weather information.

HM Coastguard Maritime Rescue Centres (MRCCs)

Aberdeen	01224 592334	Liverpool	01519 313341
Belfast	02891 463933	Milford Haven	01646 699600
Brixham	01803 882704	Portland	01305 760439
Clyde	01475 729988	Shetland	01595 692976
Dover	01304 210008	Solent	02392 552100
Falmouth	01326 310800	Stornoway	01851 702013
Forth	01333 450666	Swansea	01792 366534
Holyhead	01407 762051	Thames	01255 675518
Humber	01262 672317	Yarmouth	01493 851338

This ICS NAV5plus Navtex receiver from McMurdo provides a print out of the weather forecast on board.

Weather fax

You may find a weather fax single side band (SSB) receiver on board – this provides synoptic charts which, with practice, give you an ability to interpret approaching weather systems.

Other forecast sources

Of course there are lots of ways of getting forecasts. Yacht clubs, marinas or harbourmasters' offices often post up weather forecasts, but check these to make sure they are up-to-date.

The local TV, radio and newspapers and teletext can all be good sources of weather information.

If you know any local professional fishermen, ask them for advice; their years of experience will have made them weather-wise.

Bad weather

Your skipper will usually have some prior knowledge of bad weather but you need to be prepared for the unexpected.

Fog

A fog bank may suddenly appear even on a fine August afternoon so you need to be prepared to take action. The skipper or navigator must immediately try to fix position using visible landmarks and the crew have to be alert.

Fortunately this yacht is moored up for the night so the skipper doesn't need to worry about this sudden fog caused by warm air being cooled by contact with the cooler sea surface.

Safety in fog

- The greatest danger is that of collision with another boat so all the crew need to assist in keeping a good lookout.
- Listen for fog signals or the sound of other boats' engines.
- A crew member should be positioned in the bow, away from your own engine noise.
- The engine should be shut off periodically to listen for any boat noise or fog signals.
- All the crew should don lifejackets.
- Hoist the radar reflector.
- Put on the navigation lights.
- Monitor the echo sounder to avoid running aground.
- Sound one long blast of the horn every two minutes when motoring and two blasts when stopped.
- Maintain a steady course and speed. Your skipper may decide to either stay out in deep water or go further inshore and drop anchor until the fog clears.

Gales

If gales are expected the skipper will reduce the area of the mainsail by reefing (see page 36) and may set a small headsail such as a storm jib.

- All deck gear should be securely tied down and all loose items below deck should be put away.
- Check that all hatches are secure and the washboards are in position.
- Prepare some flasks of hot drinks and help to make sandwiches and find snacks to hand out later.
- You may need to consider whether to take seasickness pills or not.

A lee shore

This is one of a skipper's worst nightmares: being close to a shore with a strong wind blowing on to it. However skilful the helmsman is, it is possible for the boat to be blown on to the shore and wrecked! It is better to alter your route than to risk carrying on your passage close to a lee shore.

Heavy seas can quickly build up in shallow waters so the skipper may decide to stay out at sea in rough weather rather than try to anchor or risk entering a harbour with an unsheltered approach. It is a difficult decision to make, especially if night is falling and the crew are tired cold and hungry; the skipper will need your full support and realisation of the risks involved.

10 rules of the road

The International Regulations for Preventing Collisions at Sea (usually known as the Colregs for short) act like the Highway Code used for safety on our roads.

As a crew member you have to take some responsibility for avoiding a collision when sailing so you need to know at least the basic Colregs. There should be a full set of the rules carried on the boat; many sailing course books, such as *Yachtmaster for Sail and Power* (Adlard Coles Nautical) have these rules as an appendix. Here are some basics that you should learn.

Keeping a lookout

Probably the most important rule is Rule 5: 'Every vessel shall at *all times* maintain a proper lookout by sight and hearing as well as by all available means appropriate in the prevailing circumstances and conditions …'

You will probably be asked by your skipper to take a turn keeping lookout from time to time but you should get into the habit of doing this anyway when on the boat. Other more experienced crew may at times be preoccupied perhaps with sail changing and not be fully aware of other boat movements. So you can provide a very valuable contribution to the safety of the boat by keeping watch for any potential collision risks. You should be especially careful if visibility is poor. Also if the boat is heeling, you must keep a good lookout to leeward as the headsail can obscure the helmsman's vision in this direction.

As well as watching out for other boats, report any buoys, floating debris or lobster pot markers. Don't ever be afraid to mention something which you think might be a danger to the boat!

At night time watch out for very small unlit boats, unlit buoys and any fixed or flashing lights or the lights of anchored boats.

Is there a risk of collision?

Rule 7 Risk of collision states that if there is any doubt, then a risk of collision is deemed to exist. So if you are worried that you are on a collision course with an approaching vessel then compass bearings must be taken. If the compass bearings do not alter substantially then the risk of collision exists.

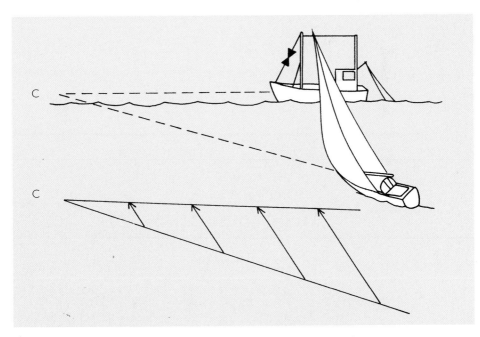

▲ *If the bearing of the fishing boat remains constant, collision will occur at C.*

Avoiding action

Rule 8 says 'Any action taken to avoid collision shall, if the circumstances of the case permit, be positive, made in ample time and with due regard to the observance of good seamanship.' In other words you should make a *positive alteration* of about 40 degrees; *ample time* (for a sailing boat): about 5 minutes; *good seamanship*: don't cross ahead of another boat. Always travel at a safe speed for the prevailing weather conditions and traffic density so that you have plenty of time to take avoiding action.

Be prepared to slow down if the visibility deteriorates or when other boats are nearby. Also you need to be able to speed up at times (by using the engine); for example a sailing boat is required to start its engine if it is travelling at less than 3 knots when crossing a shipping lane.

Sailing boats

In the Colregs, the boat with right of way is the *stand-on vessel* and the boat which needs to keep out of the way is the *give-way vessel*.

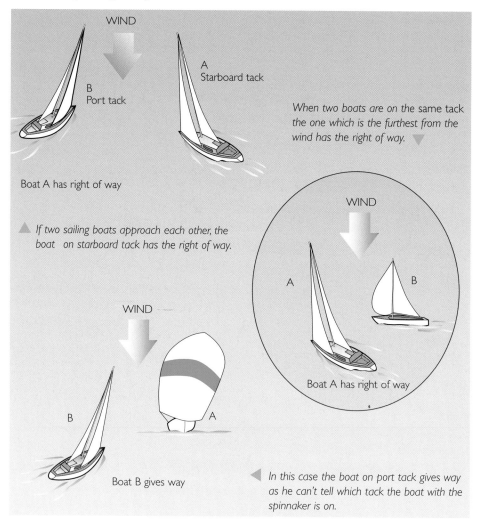

WIND

A
Starboard tack

B
Port tack

When two boats are on the same tack the one which is the furthest from the wind has the right of way. ▼

Boat A has right of way

▲ If two sailing boats approach each other, the boat on starboard tack has the right of way.

WIND

A

B

Boat A has right of way

WIND

B

A

Boat B gives way

◄ In this case the boat on port tack gives way as he can't tell which tack the boat with the spinnaker is on.

Boats under power

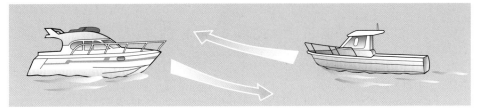

▲ In a head-on situation *neither boat has right of way; both boats need to turn to starboard.*

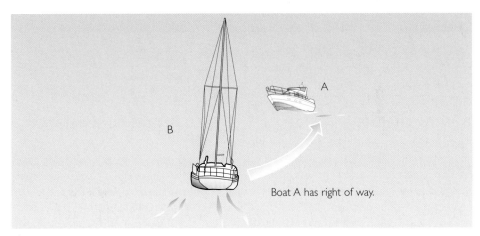

Boat A has right of way.

▲ When there is a risk of collision, the vessel which has the other on the starboard side has to give way and go astern of the other vessel.

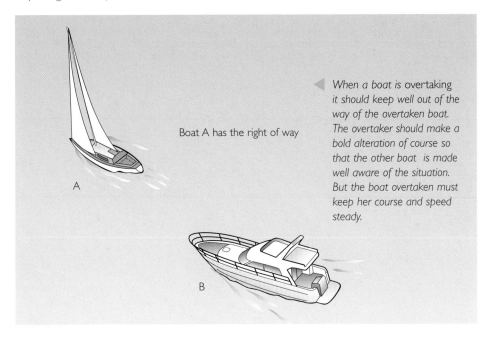

Boat A has the right of way

◄ When a boat is overtaking it should keep well out of the way of the overtaken boat. The overtaker should make a bold alteration of course so that the other boat is made well aware of the situation. But the boat overtaken must keep her course and speed steady.

It is your responsibility as a small craft to avoid shipping in major traffic lanes.

obstructs a clear view, sound one long blast on your horn and listen for a reply.

Do not anchor your boat near or in a channel.

Narrow channels

If a boat is going along a narrow channel she should keep over to the starboard side.

Sailing boats and those of less than 20 metres in length must not impede the passage of a vessel which can only navigate in the channel. This means that if there is sufficient depth of water outside the main channel for your boat then you need to keep out of the main channel. Always cross the channel at right angles.

When approaching a bend in a river which

Crossing a traffic separation scheme

Around headlands or in major shipping channels, large vessels are confined to special traffic lanes which are marked on the chart.

If you have to cross these lanes, you need to do so as quickly as possible at right angles. Don't forget that the progress of the boat will be affected by tidal streams.

There are also inshore traffic zones which smaller boats can use.

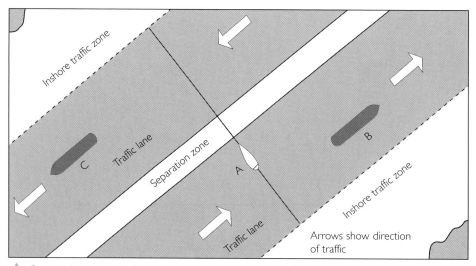

▲ Crossing shipping lanes. Boat A must cross as quickly as possible at right angles to the vessels using the traffic lanes (boats B and C).

Lights and shapes

A sailor needs to know what lights to show on his boat at night and also to be able to identify other boats' lights too.

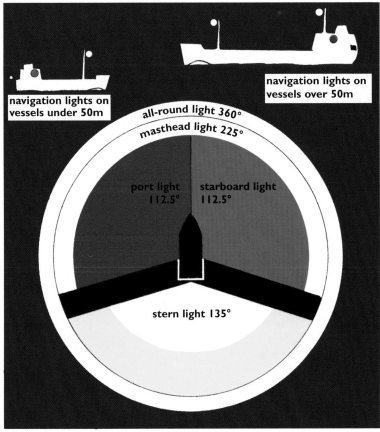

navigation lights on vessels over 50m

navigation lights on vessels under 50m

all-round light 360°

masthead light 225°

port light 112.5°   starboard light 112.5°

stern light 135°

An easy way to remember the arcs of the navigation lights is that the stern light covers an arc made up of the first three odd numbers – 1, 3, 5 – 135°. Subtract this from 360° and you have the arc of the masthead light – 225°. Halve this and you have the arcs of the port and starboard lights – 112.5°. The all-round light is 360°.

A boat under sail less than 20 metres in length can either have a tri-colour light at the mast head which shows red to port and green to starboard (see diagram) and white at the stern sector or lower side and stern lights. A vessel towing also shows a yellow light at the stern.

You could have port and starboard lights combined and mounted at the bow with a separate white light on the stern; or you could mount the three lights separately. Most small sailing yachts tend to have a combined masthead light which saves on battery power – but a bit awkward if a bulb blows!

TIP

Small boats

Watch out at night for very small sailing or power boats (under 7 metres). Under way they should display an all-round white light – but it is not obligatory and they may only have a torch!

Power driven vessels under way

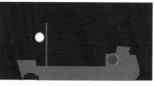

bow view of vessel
less than 50m

port

stern

bow view of vessel
more than 50m

the number of masthead lights – two compulsory
over 50m but only one compulsory under 50m –
indicate the vessel's length whatever her type

stern

Towing and pushing

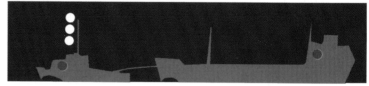

bow

tug less than 50m with length of tow more than 200m

day signal

bow tug more
than 50m

stern view, any
length

tug more than 50m with length of tow more than 200m

Fishing vessels

bow of trawler
not making way

port side of trawler more than 50m
making way

day signal

not making way

surface net fishing vessel
making way – port side

stern making way

bow not
making way

making way – port side, nets
extending more than 150m
from vessel

stern making way
(additional light
shows direction
of gear)

day signal

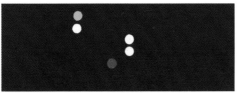

bow

trawler less than 50m making way and
shooting nets – port side

stern (additional lights
show direction of
gear)

Vessels not under command or restricted in their ability to manoeuvre

bow view – not under command

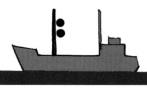

day signal (two balls)

port side – not under command but making way

bow – vessel restricted in ability to manoeuvre not making way

port side and making way

stern and making way

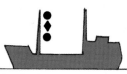

day signal

bow – vessel less than 50m, towing and unable to deviate from her course

port (same red, white, red as above)

stern

Vessels constrained by their draught

bow

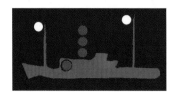

more than 50m – port side

stern

day signal

Anchored vessels and vessels aground

at anchor – more than 50m – port side

day signal

bow

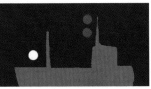

aground – less than 50m

stern

day signal

aground – more than 50m (two all round red lights plus anchor lights)

SEAPLANES

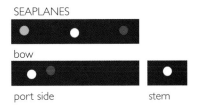

bow

port side

stern

Sound signals used when vessels are in sight of one another

Signal	Description	Meaning
●	One short blast	I am altering course to starboard
●●	Two short blasts	I am altering course to port
●●●	Three short blasts	My engines are going astern
●●●●●	Five short blasts	I am unsure of your intentions
●●●● ●	Four short blasts followed by one short blast	I intend to turn completely around to starboard
●●●● ●●	Four short blasts followed by two short blasts	I intend to turn completely around to port
— — ●	Two long blasts followed by one short blast	I wish to overtake you on your starboard side
— — ●●	Two long blasts followed by two short blasts	I wish to overtake you on your port side
— ● — ●	One long blast, one short blast, one long blast, one short blast	You may overtake me on the side indicated .

11 going into harbour

So you have had an exhilarating sail and you are now all ready to go into harbour – so what happens next?

The procedure for entering harbour has to be worked out in advance for smooth operation. If the harbour is unfamiliar then the navigator will need everyone's help in sighting landmarks and buoys, taking bearings, watching the depth and identifying leading marks or lights.

The engine starting should be checked well before the sails are taken down and you always have to be alert to the possibility of engine failure or the propeller being fouled by a rope or other detritus. The mooring lines and fenders need to be made ready.

Lowering the sails

The skipper decides on which sail to lower first. The main thing is that the boat is fully under control as it approaches harbour.

The mainsail

The boat is pointed into the wind to make lowering the mainsail easier and make it less likely to get fouled on the rigging.

Uncleat the mainsheet and kicking strap and tension the topping lift so that it takes the weight of the boom. Uncleat the main halyard and lower the sail. Unfasten the halyard from the head of the sail and secure it in its harbour stowage. Take up any slack and cleat the other end of the halyard; coil the remainder and hang the coil on the cleat. Haul in and cleat the mainsheet then tighten the kicking strap.

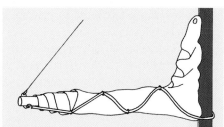

Fold mainsail over boom. Secure with shock cord.

▲ *Securing the mainsail.*

Depending on how long you are staying and how the weather is looking, either fold the sail neatly away as shown below or stow it at the luff and the leech about a metre from the foot and double it to form an envelope (see diagram and photo). Push the rest of the sail into this and then tightly roll and secure. The luff of the sail can either be left in the mast track or removed as shown. Put the cover over the sail if you have one. The main thing is to furl the sail neatly; it is a sign of good seamanship and also makes it easier to hoist later.

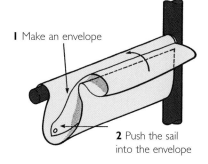

1 Make an envelope

2 Push the sail into the envelope

▲ *Stowing the mainsail.*

When stowing the mainsail you make an envelope to tidy the sail away ready to be secured.

Neatly folded mainsail ready for its cover and halyard tidied.

Stowing the mainsail in its cover.

The headsail

This is easy if your boat has a self-furling headsail, just ease off the sheet and haul in the furling line round the winch drum.

If your sail is hanked on to the forestay you lower it by first easing the halyard, letting the sail drop slowly in case it falls in the water – it will probably take two crew members: one to let down the sail and the other on the bow to gather it in.

When the sail is down, take the halyard off the head of the sail and secure it, then take up the slack and cleat it. Coil the remainder and hang it on the cleat. Then either fasten the sail to the guardrail with shock cord or put it into its bag and stow it.

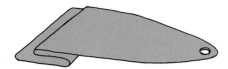

1 Lay the sail flat. Start at the foot and make a fold as shown.

2 Continue making folds until the sail is completely folded.

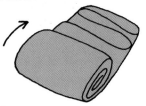

3 Roll up.

4 Stow in sail bag.

 Folding a headsail.

Preparing for berthing

The mooring lines should be made ready: secured to the deck cleats fore and aft and led through the *fairleads* (deck fittings that set the direction of the line) ready for use, see photo below. It is a good idea to tie the ends loosely to the shrouds so they are in the right position when you step off the boat but won't fall overboard and trail in the water. Fenders should be rigged in their usual places – on both sides if a change of plan is anticipated.

As the berth is approached, two crew should be ready to step off the boat with the fore and aft mooring lines.

If sufficient crew are available, the skipper will probably ask one person to stand by with a spare fender in case it is needed somewhere.

Never use your hands or feet to fend the boat off the quayside as you could be injured.

Attaching a fender – use a hitch.

Mooring lines should be secured to the deck cleats and led ashore through a fairlead.

cleat

fairlead

Coming alongside

The approach is made into the tidal stream, allowing for any wind.

Pontoon

As the boat approaches the berth, the two waiting crew members are poised ready to step on to the pontoon with the bow and stern lines, taking care not to obstruct the skipper's view. *Don't jump ashore. Wait until the boat is positioned alongside so that you only need to step across.*

Once ashore the lines are turned once round the nearby cleat or bollard to take the strain; don't pull the bow line in too far – just enough to keep the boat securely alongside. Bow and stern spring lines are then rigged (*see* page 22) to stop the boat surging back and forth with the tide. Breast lines may also be rigged for extra security.

> *Above right: This crewmember is ready with the stern line to step on to the pontoon. Fenders are in place.*
> *Below right: Stepping on to the pontoon. The fenders are well positioned to do their job.*

Quayside berth

Berthing next to a quay is much the same as by a marina pontoon but the level of the quay may be considerably higher than the boat. So the skipper will need to position the boat near a ladder on the wall. If there are posts or piles along the wall you will have to tie a plank of wood horizontally outside the fenders to protect the boat as below.

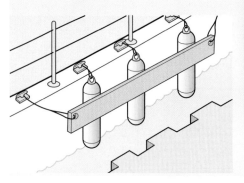

When mooring alongside a harbour wall you need to adjust the lines regularly according to the rise and fall of the tide.

Securing alongside

When you are alongside you will need to secure the boat to the side using the piles or rings while crew members climb the ladder to fasten the bow and stern lines – use bollards or cleats well forward and aft of the boat's position. They then need to rig the spring lines and breast lines if they are deemed necessary. If there is a tide rise and fall the lines must be adjusted regularly.

Bow and stern lines need to be rigged directly to the shore. When several boats are moored to the same bollard, you pass your lines through the other lines to avoid fouling them (see diagram).

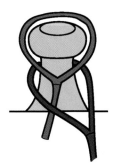

Berthing next to other boats

As soon as your boat is alongside the outer boat, the skipper may ask you to take a line and step off on to the other boat; you then take your line either fore or aft and temporarily make it fast to the fore or aft cleat on the other boat. Then spring lines need to be rigged to the other boat (see page 22); make sure that you pass the rope through fairleads to avoid chafe.

It is important to berth the boat in such a way that the spreaders don't clash if there is any swell.

When you are moored next to other boats you need to be considerate of the other boat users. Ask permission to cross other people's boats if anyone is around. Try to cross over the bow and make as little noise as possible if you come back to the boat late at night.

Leaving the boat

When all the mooring lines are secure and all spare lines are neatly coiled and stowed, there are still some jobs to do.

- Check the that the headsail and mainsail have been correctly furled or taken off and stowed if the boat is not going to be used for a while.
- Make sure that the boat is clean and ship-shape and that all loose deck items are stowed.
- All seacocks have been put in their harbour position.
- Check the bilge.
- See that the decklog has been correctly filled in.

- Check supplies of fuel, gas (make sure bottles are shut off) and water, and top up as necessary.
- Make a list of any items that need renewing and any work that needs doing before the next sail.
- Ensure that the ensign and burgee are either left hoisted or removed as appropriate (see page 94).

Make a final check on the mooring lines and fenders.

12 anchoring and mooring

This is where your job as a crew member really counts: preparing the mooring lines; being a lookout for other water users; letting the skipper or helmsperson know how close you are to the mooring or helping to select the anchoring site; being ready to pick up the mooring or let go the anchor. You need to be alert and to follow instructions closely.

Anchoring

When selecting an anchorage your skipper will be thinking about the following:

- Is there good holding ground free from obstructions?
- Does it provide maximum shelter from expected winds?
- Will your mooring area be free from obstructions when the boat swings?
- Is there sufficient depth of water to avoid going aground?
- Is it a quiet area, away from boat traffic?
- Is there somewhere to land from the dinghy?

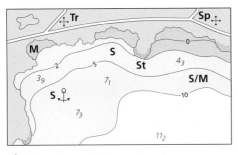

▲ *The anchor symbol on a chart shows a sheltered anchorage.*

The ideal anchorage is one where there are no other boats. A crowded area can lead to awkward situations if the wind shifts. Some of the most attractive anchorages have difficult approaches and the skipper will probably need help from the crew to find landmarks, take compass bearings and check the depth.

Approaching the anchorage

The approach to an anchorage or mooring will probably be made under power. It is important to check the strength of the tidal stream and its direction, because this will tell you the correct line of approach. Look at the mooring buoys or other boats moored in the area, as the way they are lying will show the direction and strength of the tidal stream. The skipper will make his approach in the same direction as they are lying; if it is slack water, with no tide, he will head the boat into the wind.

It is a good idea to furl the headsail to leave the foredeck clear.

A Danforth anchor secure on the bow.

Preparing to anchor

Before reaching the anchorage, feed the required length of chain or *warp* (cable) out of the anchor locker and *flake* (lay) it out on the foredeck. This ensures that the correct amount of anchor cable is ready to run out smoothly over the bow roller and won't snarl up.

Anchoring needs to be done carefully to avoid injury to the crew, especially if the anchor goes overboard accidentally. This may be obvious, but you should always check that the anchor is tied on! Letting go of the anchor and seeing it sail towards the bottom by itself is not as uncommon as you would think. Also make sure that the other end of the cable is attached to the boat!

The cable is probably marked out in five metre sections and so you can calculate how much you need to flake out, depending on the depth of water.

The pull on the anchor should be as flat along the seabed as possible, which is why about 6 metres of heavy chain is mostly used for the section attached directly to the anchor.

The anchor should be held over the bow roller ready to let go and not dangled over the bows (particularly if there is any swell).

How much cable?

The right amount of cable needed is:

+ Four times the maximum expected depth if all chain is used
+ Six times the depth if a combination of rope and chain is used
+ At least eight times the depth if you expect bad weather

Letting go of the anchor

You need to wait until the skipper gives the signal to lower the anchor; he will stop the boat and may give the engine a slight kick astern. Once the order has been given, you lift the anchor clear from the anchor roller and lower it (letting the chain and cable run cleanly over the roller) until the anchor hits the bottom. It is now important not to let the chain and line run out too quickly as it will all end up in a pile on the bottom and foul up. If there is a current running the boat will start to drift backwards, helping to lay out the cable evenly. *Make sure that you keep*

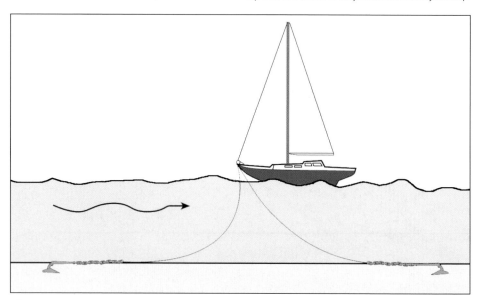

▲ *The use of two anchors will limit the boat's swinging circle.*

▲ **CQR** –*Good holding power in soft sand and mud but not so good on weed. Also known as a plough, it is hinged so it can move without breaking out.*

▲ **Danforth** – *Very good holding power on many seabed types apart from weed. It has a high power to weight ratio. It can be stored flat.*

▲ **Bruce** – *A one-piece anchor with good holding power. Because of its design, it can be used with a fairly short scope.*

▲ **Grapnel** – *A light anchor for dinghies – the folding type shown here is easy to stow.*

Always wait for the skipper's signal before lowering the anchor.

your feet and fingers clear of the running chain and cable.

Once the skipper is satisfied that the anchor is holding, the line is then secured to a cleat on the foredeck.

If you are anchoring by day it is correct to show a black anchor ball forward. If you are anchoring at night you do need to show an all-round white anchor light forward.

Is the anchor holding?

Because anchors don't always take a firm hold on the bottom immediately, it is important to check if it is dragging.

Choose two transit marks in line on the shore and watch to see if you are moving out of position.

If the boat doesn't have a winch, you can help to raise the anchor.

An electric anchor winch will make light work of weighing anchor.

Weighing anchor

This is not about measuring how heavy the anchor is but the term used to haul the anchor back in again when you are leaving.

Some boats will have a *windlass* or winch for hauling up the anchor but you may have to pull it up by hand (bend your knees!). Don't start to haul it up until the skipper tells you to – he will probably motor forward to make the line slack for you, especially if you have to haul it up by hand. If the anchor is well dug in, the skipper may need to use the engine to help to free it and also if there is a strong tidal stream. You can help him manoeuvre by indicating the lie of the anchor cable.

Once the anchor is off the bottom, tell the skipper, and let him know when it is clear of the water. Bring the anchor back on board – it might need a bit of a scrub if you have been anchored on a muddy, weedy bottom.

What do you do if the anchor is stuck?

Sometimes the anchor gets caught fast on a rock or other obstruction on the seabed. If you know the bottom is rocky it is a good idea to rig a trip line attached to the anchor with the other end marked with a buoy. Then you haul on the buoy to free the anchor.

If you don't have a trip line you can often clear the fouled anchor by motoring in the opposite direction to that in which it was laid.

If your anchor gets hooked on an under-water cable or another boat's mooring rope you can use the boathook to take the strain off the cable so you can work the anchor free.

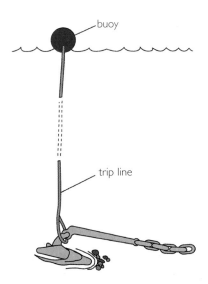

Kedge anchor

A kedge anchor is a secondary or lightweight anchor with a short length of chain and rope used for holding a boat temporarily in position in fine weather.

It can also be laid at an angle to the main anchor in strong winds to stop the boat *yawing* or swinging from side to side: the strain put on the mooring by the wind and tide is then spread on to both anchors and limits the swinging circle. The disadvantage of kedging is that unless your skipper is very skilful, you may have to row out the second anchor using the dinghy.

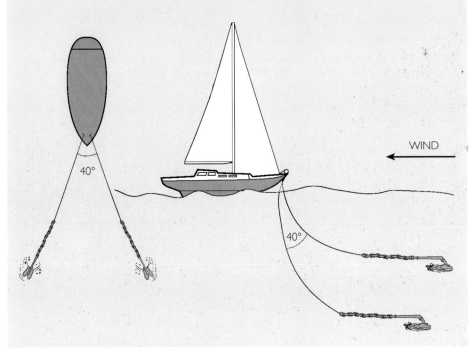

Mooring

Once your skipper has decided which mooring buoy he is aiming for he will approach it head-to-wind, or against the tidal stream.

Picking up a mooring

Moorings can vary quite a bit. Sometimes you will come across one with a ring which you use to attach your line. Generally a mooring buoy will have a smaller pick-up buoy floating nearby.

As you approach the buoy, into the tidal stream, you need to indicate the direction and distance from the buoy to the helmsman as he may not be able to see the pick-up buoy.

When the bow of the boat is alongside the buoy, you use the boathook to snag the line on the pick-up buoy and bring it on board. The line of the small buoy should be attached to a heavier mooring rope with a loop on the end. Pass this over the anchor roller and fasten it to a deck cleat.

If your mooring buoy has a ring, again use the boathook to catch the ring and hold it steady (it might be a good idea to lie down to do this) and get another crew member to pass the line through the ring and back on board, over the bow roller, to be secured with a bow-line. You could rig a separate slip line through the ring and back on board as back-up or to hold the boat steady whilst you undo the main mooring rope when leaving.

Leaving a mooring

This is much easier than mooring! If you have rigged a slip line on to a ring on the buoy, one crew can control this whilst you untie the main mooring rope. Don't cast off until the skipper tells you to.

If you have a mooring warp from a pick-up buoy on board, you can throw the pick-up buoy overboard in readiness and then, when the skipper tells you, release the mooring warp from the cleat and cast off. Let the skipper know as soon as you have done this and keep an eye on the pick-up buoy to avoid it getting fouled in the propeller.

You will need to use plenty of fenders when using a crowded mooring like this one at Seaton, Devon.

You can use your boathook to catch the pick-up buoy. This is attached to a heavier mooring rope.

If the mooring buoy has a ring on top you can pass the line through it and back on board to secure to a cleat.

Always make sure that children wear life jackets in the dinghy.

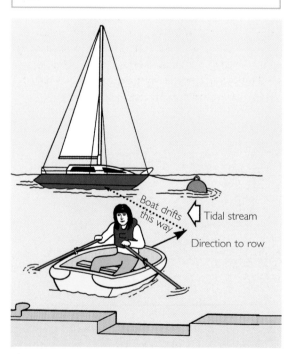

▲ *Allowing for the tidal stream.*

Using the dinghy

The boat will have some kind of dinghy or tender so that you can get ashore from a mooring or anchorage. Mostly people use inflatables these days but whatever type, the rules are the same:

♦ Wear a lifejacket, especially at night.
♦ Make sure that the dinghy is securely fastened to the boat before boarding.
♦ If there is an outboard attached, make sure it is attached to the dinghy with a line in case it slips off its bracket.
♦ Be careful to avoid fuel spillage.
♦ Have a pump (to reflate the dinghy if necessary), extra fuel, engine spares, a bailer and oars on board.
♦ Carry a torch and a VHF radio.
♦ Don't let the painter (mooring line) trail overboard in case it fouls the propeller.
♦ Never overload the dinghy.

You board the dinghy either from a ladder at the side or stern of the yacht. Never jump into a dinghy; it may capsize or the floor could be damaged. The oarsman or helm should board first, followed by the crew, stepping in carefully one at a time and distributing the weight evenly. Never stand up or make sudden movements as this can cause a capsize.

If there is a strong wind or tidal stream you will need to point the dinghy into the wind or stream. It is not as easy as you might think to drive or row an inflatable dinghy so get some boat handling practice in calm waters if you can.

As you approach the shore under power, stop the engine when it becomes shallow and tilt the engine up to avoid damage to the propeller. Be ready to jump out to prevent the dinghy from running on to rocks or going broad side to the waves. You can then all help to carry it up the beach to a safe position.

If you moor the dinghy when you get to the shore, make sure you leave a long painter to allow for the fall of the tide. The oars should be very well secured.

When launching from a beach, walk the dinghy to rowing depth and get in. If you are using an outboard, make sure you have sufficient depth of water before you lower the pro-

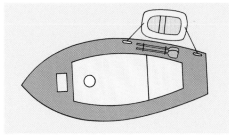

▲ *Securing the dinghy alongside.*

Emergency dinghy power
If you get engine failure on the yacht, you can secure a powered dinghy with springs, bow and stern lines alongside as an auxiliary engine to give emergency propulsion. This works better than trying to tow the boat from the bow.

peller into the water. Don't stand near the stern when the motor is being started.

Back at the boat you can either deflate the dinghy and stow it on board or secure it alongside (see diagram). Except in very calm weather it is not a good idea to tow a dinghy behind the boat as it could capsize.

A neat inflatable dinghy pack from Zodiac with boat, oars, inflator and repair kit.

13 flags and sailing etiquette

Flag etiquette

A cruising boat is 'properly dressed' when she is flying a masthead burgee and her national ensign.

Burgee

This is a small triangular flag which shows the insignia of the sailing club of which the owner of the boat is a member.

Ensign

Ensigns are national maritime flags which are worn at all times when at sea. In harbour it is hoisted at 0800 in summer and 0900 in winter and lowered at sunset or 2100 whichever is the earlier. The ensign is not worn by yachts when racing.

Courtesy ensign

When visiting a foreign country, your own ensign should be flown at the stern and the ensign of the country being visited is flown from the starboard spreader during your stay. This is known as a courtesy ensign.

House flag

This is a rectangular private flag of the boat's owner flown from the starboard spreader. If you need to fly a courtesy flag from this spreader then the house flag goes on the port spreader.

International code flags

These are internationally agreed signals designed for communication between ships before the days of radio and electronic aids.

A set of signal flags consists of 26 rectangular or swallow-tailed letter flags, 10 numeral pennants, three substitutes (one of 3 triangular two-coloured flags flown to repeat a letter or number higher in the same *hoist*, or group of flags).

Naval ensign (White ensign)

Civil ensign (Red ensign)

Blue ensign

HM Customs and Excise ensign

▲ *Some British ensigns.*

ANSWERING PENNANT

A – Alpha

I have a diver down: keep well clear at slow speed

B – Bravo

I am taking in, or discharging or carrying dangerous goods

C – Charlie

Yes, affirmative

D – Delta

Keep clear of me: I am manoeuvring with difficulty

E – Echo

I am altering my course to starboard

F – Foxtrot

I am disabled: communicate with me

G – Golf

I require a pilot.
Flown by *fishing vessels*
I am hauling in nets

H – Hotel

I have a pilot on board

I – India

I am altering my course to port

J – Juliet

I am on fire and have dangerous cargo: keep well clear of me

K – Kilo

I wish to communicate with you

L – Lima

You should stop your vessel instantly

M – Mike

My vessel is stopped and making no way through the water

N – November

No, negative

O – Oscar

Man overboard

P – Papa

Vessel about to put to sea
Flown by *fishing vessels*
My nets are caught fast

Q – Quebec

My vessel is 'healthy' and I request free practice*

R – Romeo

S – Sierra

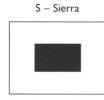

My engines are going astern

T – Tango

Keep clear of me; I am engaged in pair trawling

U – Uniform

You are running into danger

V – Victor

I require assistance

W – Whiskey

I require medical assistance

X – X-ray

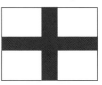

Stop carrying out your intentions and watch for my signals

Y – Yankee

I am dragging my anchor

Z – Zulu

I require a tug
Flown by *fishing vessels*
I am shooting nets

FIRST SUBSTITUTE

SECOND SUBSTITUTE

THIRD SUBSTITUTE

1

2

3

4

5

6

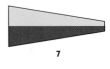

7

8

9

0

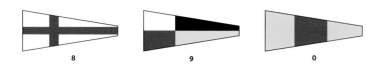

*A certificate showing that the boat has been released from quarantine.

Dressing a boat overall

This term describes a boat in harbour which has the set of international code flags hoisted on a line from the very front of the bow to the top of the mast and down to the stern. Dressing overall is done to celebrate some special occasion such as the Queen's birthday or a club regatta day.

Sailing etiquette

Good manners usually come naturally to sailors but there are a few dos and don'ts to remember:

+ When berthing next to another boat, always ask permission to come alongside if there is someone on board.
+ If you are rafted up and have to cross another boat to get ashore, always cross their fore-deck making as little noise as possible, especially late at night. Ask permission if anyone is about. Be careful not to put undue pressure on any fittings.
+ When motoring in busy waterways, always be courteous to others afloat, whatever craft they are using.
+ When overtaking smaller or anchored boats make sure that your wash does not disturb them.
+ On inland waterways, again make sure that you respect the comfort of crew on moored boats and don't rush to get ahead of other boats to enter locks. Help others with lock gates where necessary.

Help the environment

Keeping your environment free from rubbish and water pollution is a responsibility that applies to all yachtsmen.

+ Keep all your litter on board (even biodegradable material) until you arrive at the next harbour and dispose of it in the bins provided.
+ Do not discharge a sea toilet in a harbour unless you have a holding tank.
+ Do not dump any toxic chemicals such as anti-foul, paint or engine oil at sea.

14 safety afloat

You should take great care when moving around the boat as there are many trip hazards and sharp items of equipment which can be dangerous. Always wear substantial footwear and make sure that you have a safe handhold (avoid grabbing the stanchions and guardrails, use the shrouds instead).

Safety harnesses

In rough weather and at night, everyone on deck should wear a safety harness which should be clipped on to a strong deck fitting or a lifeline running the length of the deck. Make sure you are shown where to clip yours on.

When moving along the deck, keep your body low and hold on to grabrails where you can. It is better to walk along the up-sloping side of the deck so that if you do lose your balance, the tendency will be to roll towards the centre of the boat and not off it.

Lifejackets

Everyone on board should be allocated a lifejacket and know where it is stowed. They should always be worn:

* In thick fog
* In severe weather
* When going ashore in the dinghy
* By all non-swimmers
* If the boat has to be abandoned

Lifejackets are brightly coloured orange or yellow so that they can be seen easily; most now also have retro-reflective strips so that a casualty can be seen in the water at night. Lifejackets also have whistles and may have waterproof lights.

This crew is wearing sensible footwear, a lifejacket and is safely holding on to a shroud.

▲ *Self inflating Crewsaver lifejacket with harness.*

If heavy weather is expected wear your harness and know where to clip on.

Make sure that your lifejacket is adjusted comfortably over the clothes you are wearing and know how it operates.

Make sure that your jacket fits correctly over the clothes you will be wearing on the boat or it will not support you adequately in the water.

The basic type is made of foam but may have the facility for additional buoyancy by mouth inflation. Inflatable lifejackets are inflated via a CO_2 cartridge (replaceable) with back-up oral inflation; some inflate automatically when immersed whilst others are pull-tab operated. Ask to be shown how yours works. A good lifejacket is designed to float an unconscious person face up.

If you decide to buy your own, look for a jacket that conforms to the BS EN 395:194 standard with a minimum buoyancy rating of 100N (Newtons). Sometimes you will see jackets referred to as PFDs which means Personal Flotation Devices. Buoyancy aids are not the same as a lifejacket; they are soft, foam filled waistcoats which will just assist flotation. These are generally used for watersports such as water skiing and have insufficient buoyancy for general sailing use.

Useful extras

Many sailors carry a knife of some sort to cut rope in an emergency. You can get a waterproof strobe to attach to your jacket which emits a powerful flash with high visibility. There are also personal locator beacons (PLBs) available now which use satellite technology to summon the search and rescue services.

15 emergencies

Safety training will help to minimise danger but if an incident happens at sea, you will need to know the emergency procedures.

Man overboard

Every crew member should be able to assist in a man overboard situation and act quickly. The most experienced able-bodied crew member will be at the helm but there is much you can do to help:

Immediate crew action for man overboard

1 If someone falls overboard you shout 'man overboard' straight away to alert all the crew and the skipper who will press the MOB button on the GPS.
2 Throw the lifebuoy (and the danbuoy if carried) towards the casualty in the water. If it is at night, activate the light before throwing.
3 Point continuously at the person in the water calling out his relative position to the boat and distance off. *Do not take your eyes off him*. In a rough sea or at night he could be lost to view very quickly.
4 If visibility is poor, throw in other floating objects which can form a trail which can be followed when the boat turns round and heads back.
5 The skipper will sheet in the mainsail and start the engine for the pick up. Once he is under power he will call for the headsail to be furled.
6 Check that no lines are trailing over the side which could snag the propeller.
7 Make a note of the time, course and log reading in case the person is lost to sight and it is necessary to make a search pattern.

If someone falls overboard keep the person in sight constantly and direct the helmsman.

Whether you use sail or power for recovering the MOB, the objective is to get back to the person quickly and stop the boat alongside him or her. In cold water, survival time is counted in minutes not hours.

A life ring with dan buoy which has a flag to help identify the spot where the casualty went overboard. It should be stowed within easy reach of the helmsman so he can drop it instantly.

The skipper will probably practise one or two MOB drills using a fender as the casualty, probably under power. However in an emergency, with engine failure, it may have to be done under sail so ask him to practise that method with you. Also ask to be shown how to heave-to. The skipper steers so the bow turns through the wind and the jib is 'backed'. This pushes the bow further so the wind is on the beam, stopping forward movement.

amount of skill and will also take the boat a distance away from the person in the water.

When running in light airs or if only a headsail is set, this method is preferable and the boat may be gybed round.

Under power

Immediately heave-to and start the engine. Lower the sails. If you are short-handed, drop the mainsail and let the headsail fly.

Make sure that no sheets are trailing in the water. When the boat reaches the person in the water and he is secured, the engine *must be stopped* to avoid injury by the propeller.

In an emergency, this method is within the capabilities of an inexperienced person provided they have been shown how to heave-to.

If the MOB incident happens from a power boat, steer the boat so that the propeller is away from the casualty in the water. Turn a fairly tight circle to come alongside, with the boat head-to-wind.

MOB recovery methods

Sailing

Whatever point of sailing the boat is on, immediately go on to a reach and sail away (5 to 7 boat lengths) from the person in the water to enable the boat to reverse course and return under full control. When the boat is ready, tack round on to the opposite reach and sail back along the previous track. Make the final approach on a close reach with both sails flying so that the boat can be stopped with the person to leeward ready for the pick up.

Using this method, the boat is fully under control and the crew have time to organise themselves but it does require a certain

The pick up

It is very difficult to lift a waterlogged person out of the water, especially if they are unconscious. Whilst the boat is returning to the casualty, prepare the rescue ring with a buoyant line attached to the boat. Alternatively, prepare a loop in a line with a bowline knot. When you are alongside the casualty, secure the free end of the line to the boat and pass the loop over his head and shoulders if he is too weak to help himself; if he is able, he can put his foot in it to get leverage. If there is a boarding or swim ladder at the stern float him round to it, ensuring that the engine is stopped.

If the casualty is unconscious, it may be necessary for another crew member to go into the water to secure a rope round him. That person *must* wear a lifejacket and have a separate lifeline attached to the boat.

Lifting out

If there are insufficient crew, or the casualty is too heavy to lift manually, attach one of sail halyards to him and use the winch.

Another method is to clip the luff of the jib on to the guardrail; lower the bight of the sail into the water and float it under him. Then attach the halyard to the clew of the sail and winch him out of the water.

If the casualty is unconscious or injured, you may have to resort to inflating the dinghy and getting him into it to assist onboard recovery.

If the MOB victim has been recovered unconscious and has suffering near drowning, he will need urgent medical attention even if he appears to recover well. This is because secondary drowning can set in several hours later due to irritation in the lungs from the sea water; this can cause dangerous amounts of fluid to build up.

Liferafts

It is important that everyone on board knows how to launch, inflate and board the liferaft.

Don't launch the liferaft until you are ready to use it as it may capsize in rough seas.

Before abandoning

◆ Send out a distress call giving your position.
◆ Put on plenty of warm clothing; top with foul weather gear and your lifejacket and harness.
◆ Collect the grab bag (a bag kept ready packed with items such as torch, a sharp knife, hand-held VHF radio flares, signalling mirror and food and drink.)
◆ If there is one on board, take the EPIRB (Emergency Position Indicating Radio Beacon).

Launching

◆ Make sure the painter is secured to a strong point on the yacht.
◆ Release the fastenings which secure the liferaft to the boat and launch it, keeping clear of the painter.
◆ When it is in the water, pull in the painter and give it a sharp tug to inflate the raft.

One of the first exercises you will learn as crew is MOB. It is hard to haul a real casualty on board but when practising you will only have to retrieve a dan buoy or a fender.

Boarding

+ Do not jump into the liferaft; board it from the ladder or from the sea. The heaviest and strongest person should board first.
+ Once everyone is on board, cut the painter and paddle clear of the yacht.

On the liferaft

+ Stream the drogue (a sea anchor shaped like a cone).
+ Position everyone evenly to avoid capsize.
+ Close up the entrance to the raft.
+ Activate the EPIRB (if available).
+ Check that everyone is OK – treat any injuries.

+ Open the survival pack and take out the first aid kit, flares and seasickness tablets. Make sure you reseal the pack after use.
+ Send a Mayday on the VHF radio as soon as possible and send distress messages at regular intervals – until you get a reply.
+ Check the raft for air leaks.
+ Try to avoid drinking water for the first 24 hours (unless injured and losing blood) as supplies will be limited.
+ Do not drink sea water or urine.
+ Make sure everyone keeps warm.
+ Post a look out and arrange watches.
+ Try to estimate your position
+ Give everyone a task to keep them focussed and encourage them with positive thinking.

An Avon six person liferaft.

Collision

Traditionally, the safety of the boat comes first because if it sinks then everyone is in extreme danger.

If a boat has been in a collision, the immediate priority is to try to control the flooding. Once the situation is stabilised and the boat is no longer in danger of sinking, or catching fire, then any injuries can be treated.

To stop a flood, push soft items such as blankets, sleeping bags, pillows and cushions into the hole from the inside and, if possible drape a sail over the hole from the outside.

It is said that a frightened person with a bucket is the best way of emptying a boat full of water, but in reality the bilge pump is your best bet. The toilet pump can also be used if a length of tubing is fed from the bilges into the toilet. The hose from the engine cooling system could possibly be disconnected and placed in the bilges. When the engine is run, water will be sucked up through it and discharged overboard.

Fire

If a fire breaks out on board the first thing to do is to shout 'FIRE' to alert everyone on board to the danger. Move everything combustible out of the way, if you can do so safely and take immediate action to extinguish the flames.

Fire needs three elements to spread so these need to be removed:

Fuel	Cut off the fuel source by turning off the gas and removing gas cylinders, fuel containers, cooking oil etc away from the area of the fire.
Oxygen	Starve the fire of oxygen by smothering it; use fire extinguishers or a fire blanket.
Heat	Cool the fire by attacking the base of it with a fire extinguishing medium.

Fire extinguishers

Fire extinguishers are coded with a letter and a number denoting the category and size of fire for which they are suitable. Those approved to European standard will carry a BS EN3 certification mark.

The most likely fire extinguisher you will find on board will be dry powder which, although very messy, can deal with all types of fire safely. There may also be a CO_2 extinguisher which can be used for electrical fires, gases and flammable liquids but care must be taken as there is a risk of suffocation in small spaces. Foam extinguishers can be used for paper, wood and textiles, flammable liquids but is not suitable for electrical fires.

Water can be used for damping down fabrics and is effective on wood but must not be used on electrical, fuel or hot fat fires.

This is a 2kg ABC coded dry powder fire extinguisher which can deal with all types of fire.

Fire blankets

One of the most common sources of fire is a pan catching alight. If this happens, turn off the gas, don't move the pan but smother the fire with a fire blanket or a heavy damp cloth.

Wrap your knuckles in the edge of the blanket and lay it over the fire away from you so as not to fan the flames towards you.

Never pour water onto a pan fire or throw it overboard in case the fire spreads.

Taking action

When using a fire extinguisher, make sure you know how to operate it; don't put yourself in danger and have a clear exit from the fire zone. Tell the other crewmembers to go up on deck.

If the fire seems to be getting out of control, inflate the dinghy and tow it astern; see that the liferaft is ready; put on lifejackets and have one of the crew standing by to send a distress alert.

Fire safety

* Don't smoke on board.
* Don't store fuel below decks.
* Don't leave pans unattended on the stove.
* Check electrical wiring regularly.
* Fit a smoke detector near the galley and the engine.
* Keep the bilges clean

Using gas on board

When using gas cylinders on board, follow these guidelines:
* See that all fittings are correctly installed and that there are no leaks.
* Check for chafe on the rubber hoses.
* Stow gas cylinders in a container in the cockpit which drains overboard.
* When not in use, turn off the gas from the cylinder; burn the gas out of the pipes and turn off at the cooker.
* Do not leave a lit cooker unattended.
* After replacing a cylinder, check for leaks by smearing the joint between the valve and the bottle with soapy water. If bubbles appear then there is a leak.

Accidents and first aid

Before leaving harbour the skipper should check whether anyone is likely to need special medical attention or is on any medication. Every crew member should be able to treat minor ailments and, in the event of a more serious accident, be able to make the patient as comfortable as possible so that injuries may be contained until help arrives.

Hypothermia

Anyone who is rescued from cold water will probably be suffering from a reduced core body temperature or hypothermia. This should be treated urgently as there is a risk of death.

Symptoms:
* Cold and shivering violently
* Rapid shallow breathing
* Pallor and lips, fingers and toes become blue
* Irritability or unnatural quietness
* Lack of co-ordination and energy
* Collapse

Treatment:
* Prevent further heat loss straight away by protecting him from the wind and weather. Get him below and wrap him in blankets or a sleeping bag. If an exposure or 'space' blanket is available (plastic sheet with a reflective surface), wrap this around him to contain body heat.
* Monitor the patient constantly. Check pulse and breathing rate.
* **Do not allow the patient to be vertical** (blood will drain from the core to the legs)
* **Do not give food, alcohol or other drinks** (the body will divert blood to the stomach to aid digestion and reduce the core temperature further)
* **Do not massage or rub the body**

With any cases of severe hypothermia the patient must be referred to hospital for medical assessment.

Injuries	
Small cuts	Wash and cleanse with antiseptic and cover with a plaster or dressing.
Burns & scalds	Immediately flood the affected area with cold water for at least 10 minutes then leave open or cover with a clean, dry dressing.
Bleeding	Apply and maintain pressure to the wound with fingers or a pad of clean cloth. Bandage with a clean, dry dressing firmly but not too tightly. If blood soaks through the first dressing, apply another over the top. If blood loss continues, reapply the dressing. If there are no fractures, raise the limb to reduce blood flow. Lay patient down and treat for shock.
Bruises	Apply a cold compress.
Dislocations & Fractures	Do not move the patient unless necessary. Immobilise the limb – if it is a leg gently but firmly bandage the legs together to split the fracture. Keep patient warm; watch for signs of shock.
Seasickness	Give the patient something to do on deck which requires concentration. If they are badly affected send them below to lie down.
Headache	Give paracetamol or aspirin (with a little food to protect the stomach lining).
Sunburn	Cool with calamine lotion or cream containing aloe vera. Cover up to prevent further burning.
Strains & sprains	Apply a cold compress or ice pack if available, elevate the limb to reduce swelling. Give anti-inflamatory medicine such as ibuprofen.

Shock

You should look for symptoms of shock for all injuries.

Symptoms:

The patient appears pale, his skin feels clammy; he may be perspiring; breathing may be fast and shallow; he may start yawning and sighing; he may vomit, be thirsty or over-anxious.

▲ *Lay the patient down and raise the legs.*

Treatment:

Lay the patient down and raise and support the legs; Keep him warm by covering with a blanket or sleeping bag. Check the pulse and breathing regularly. Do not give food or drink. Comfort and reassure the patient.

Head injuries

All head injuries are potentially very serious and need professional assessment but the patient should be monitored carefully. After any bleeding head wounds have been dealt with watch for the following symptoms and make a note of them to pass on to a qualified health practitioner:

♦ Drowsiness
♦ Dizziness
♦ Dilated pupils
♦ Garbled speech
♦ Loss of memory

- Headache
- Bleeding from the ears or nose (especially if patient has been unconscious)

Fluid in the brain cavity or a depressed bone from the injury may be compressing the brain and the patient can lapse into a coma. Seek medical help as quickly as possible.

Resuscitation

When breathing has stopped it is necessary to start resuscitation. Unless this is done within four minutes, brain damage may occur.

Expired air resuscitation (EAR)

1 Lay the patient on his back.
2 Clear his mouth of obstructions and check that his tongue is not blocking the airway

3 Tilt his head back and lift the jaw as shown below to ensure a clear airway.
4 Pinch his nose firmly take a good breath and blow into his mouth (or close the mouth with your thumb and blow into his nose). Ensure that you have a good seal. Look along his chest to make sure it rises. If it doesn't then check your seal.
5 Turn your head away, wait for his chest to fall; take a fresh breath and repeat. Initially give five breaths and then one every four seconds.
6 Continue until he is breathing normally or until a medical expert can take over.
7 Once normal breathing is resumed, place in the recovery position (see below) and monitor him carefully in case his breathing stops again.

Left: tilt the head back and lift the jaw to clear the airway.
Right: Ideally two people should administer EAR and CPR.

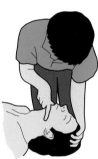

First aid kit

The first aid kit should be kept in a watertight box and the contents listed on the outside of the box. The following items should be found in a basic first aid kit:

Roll of sticking plaster	Paracetamol
Individual sticking plaster	Ibruprofen
Large triangular bandage	Seasickness tablets
Small bandages	Exposure bag (space
Lint	blanket)
Cotton wool	First aid manual
Scissors	
Tweezers	
Safety pins	
Eye lotion and eye bath	
Calomine lotion	
Antiseptic	

Cardio-pulmonary resuscitation (CPR)

If the victim's heart stops beating then full cardio-pulmonary resuscitation (CPR) should be carried out with chest compressions. This should be applied by a trained first aider for a successful outcome as there may be a weak pulse which is hard to detect. Essentially, the action is as follows:

- The heel of the hand is placed in the centre of the chest.
- The other hand is placed over the top and the fingers interlocked.
- Keeping the arms straight, pressure is applied to the chest to depress it about 4-5cms and released.
- This is repeated 30 times at about 100 per minute.

This will need to be done in conjunction with EAR at a rate of 30 compressions to two breaths. If you start CPR you are committed to carrying on until a medical professional arrives on the scene.

Recovery position

An unconscious patient who is breathing steadily and does not have a life-threatening condition (such as a spinal injury or severe bleeding) should be placed in the recovery position which will protect him from choking if he vomits:

- Gently roll the patient on to his side.
- Lift the chin forward to give a clear airway.
- Place the patient's hand under the cheek to elevate the mouth and chin.
- Bring the right knee forward to stabilise the body.
- Monitor pulse and breathing continuously. Do not leave the patient unattended.
- If the recovery position is needed for more than half an hour, turn the body on to the other side if safe to do so.

Even if the patient appears to recover from unconsciousness, seek medical help as soon as possible.

Distress

All crew members must know the distress procedures and the use of flares. A distress signal is only used when there is a grave and imminent danger to the boat or crew. You need to know the 10 internationally recognised distress signals:

Distress signals

1 Continuous sounding of the fog horn.
2 The morse letters SOS by light or sound
3 The word Mayday on the radio
4 International code flags N over C
5 A square shape above or below a round shape
6 A red rocket parachute flare or red hand flare
7 An orange smoke signal by day
8 Outstretched arms slowly and repeatedly raised and lowered
9 Flames on the boat
10 An explosive device

▲ Some visual distress and safety signals at sea.

Pyrotechnics (Flares)

Orange smoke: A daytime distress signal which produces a dense cloud of orange smoke which can be easily seen from the air. In strong winds, however, the smoke blows along the sea surface and may not be visible from the shore or other boats.

Handheld smokes burn for about 50 seconds and are used when rescuers are in sight. Buoyant canister smokes (activated with a ring-pull) burn for three minutes.

Red hand-held flare: This is used when you are within sight of land or another boat, or to pinpoint your position when rescuers are within visible range; it will burn for about 40 seconds.

Do not point it into the wind or you will be covered with sparks and smoke. Point it outboard and do not look directly at it.

1 Remove plastic lid
2 Tear off foil cover
3 Pull cord firmly
4 Throw cannister overboard downwind

▲ Operating an orange smoke signal.

Red parachute rocket flare: This type of flare is used when out of sight of land. It launches a very bright red parachute-suspended flare to a height of 300m and burns for 40 seconds.

It should be fired vertically or, in strong winds, 15 degrees downwind. If there is low cloud it should be fired 45 degrees downwind so that the flare ignites below the cloud base.

White hand-held flare: This is not used for distress but to warn other boats of your position. It burns for 50 seconds. Do not look directly at it.

This flare pack is intended for day or night use up to 7 miles from land. It contains 2 red hand-flares, 2 parachute red rockets and two orange handsmokes.

I Remove top and bottom end caps

2 Remove safety pin

3 Hold flare firmly. Squeeze trigger lever. Fire vertically slightly downwind.

▲ *Operating a red rocket flare.*

Flare safety

♦ Learn the purpose of each of the flares and know how to use them.
♦ Read and memorise the operating instructions and always follow them exactly.
♦ If a flare fails, hold it in the firing position for at least 30 seconds. Remove the caps and drop it in the sea to avoid accidents on board.
♦ Never point a flare at another person.
♦ Stow in a secure, dry place which is easily accessible and make sure that all crew members know where they are located.
♦ Always have at least the minimum required number and type of flare on board and make sure that they are within their use-by date.

VHF radio

VHF (Very High Frequency) radio gives the reliable, simple communication when you are afloat but it is essentially a line-of-sight, short-range system.

Most conversations usually take place on simplex channels where only one person can speak at a time. There is a button on the set which is pressed to transmit and released to receive. The channel currently used for initial calling is channel 16 – you switch to another agreed channel once you have established contact with the person you wish to talk to. The exception is when making distress calls – you remain on channel 16.

GMDSS/DSC

The boat you are sailing on may be fitted with a DSC radio (Digital Selective Calling) which is a development of part of the Global Maritime Distress and Safety System (GMDSS). With this type of set you can instantly send an automatically formatted distress message to the Coastguard and other craft fitted with DSC sets. If the DSC radio is linked to GPS, the boat's position will be sent.

Distress calls (Mayday)

This call is made when the vessel or a crew member is in grave and imminent danger.

1 Switch on the set and select channel 16.
2 Listen to ensure that no other station is transmitting.
3 Depress the press-to-speak button and say MAYDAY slowly and clearly three times.
4 Say the words 'THIS IS' and the BOAT'S NAME three times.
5 Repeat MAYDAY and the BOAT'S NAME once.
6 Give the boat's position either as latitude and longitude, or as a bearing from and distance off a known geographical point.

TIP

Licence to call

To legally use a VHF radio on the boat you need to hold a Marine Radio Operator's Certificate. Ideally most of the crew should have this but, if you don't, in an emergency you could use the radio under the supervision of a qualified person.

This handheld ICOM VHF radio is switched to Channel 16, used for initial calling, safety and distress.

7 Give the nature of the distress (sinking, on fire etc) and assistance required.
8 Give the number of persons on board.
9 End the message with the word 'OVER'.
10 Release the press-to-talk button and wait.
11 Repeat the message if there is no reply within three minutes.

Here is an example of a distress message:

MAYDAY MAYDAY MAYDAY
This is yacht JETTO JETTO JETTO
MAYDAY yacht JETTO
My position is one five zero Beachy Head light one point five miles
I am sinking and need immediate assistance
I have four persons on board
OVER

Sending an Urgency call (Pan Pan)

This is used for a very urgent message concerning the safety of a person or a vessel. It is not yet a distress situation but may become one.

1 Switch on the set and select channel 16.
2 Listen to ensure that no other channel is transmitting.
3 Depress the press-to-speak button and say PAN PAN three times.

VHF radio is your link to friends afloat, harbour masters, marinas and most importantly, the rescue services.

4 Call anyone listening by saying the words ALL STATIONS three times.

6 Give the BOAT'S NAME three times.

7 Give the reason for the call and the help needed.

8 End the message with word OVER.

9 Press the press-to-talk button and wait for a reply.

Here is an example of an urgency message:

PAN PAN   PAN PAN   PAN PAN
All stations All stations All stations
This is yacht JETTO JETTO JETTO
My position is two seven zero from Needles Lighthouse six miles
My engine has failed
I am drifting and need a tow urgently
OVER

Medical assistance

If you have a sick crew member on board and are not sure what medical assistance he needs, advice can be obtained by making a Pan Pan call. Once the call has been answered, say that you need urgent medical advice.

The Coastguard will then contact a doctor; he will be linked to you via a working channel number which you will be given. The Coastguard will monitor the call in case immediate transportation of the patient is required.

EPIRBs

Many yachts now carry EPIRBs (Emergency Position Indicating Radio Beacon). These are essentially transmitters which, once activated send a signal containing the boat's unique code number to Falmouth Coastguard via a satellite. The Coastguard then tells the nearest rescue centre the position of the vessel in distress so a rescue can be co-ordinated.

SART

Once the EPIRB has been activated and a distress signal automatically sent, a Search and Rescue Radar Transponder (SART) can be used on board or in the liferaft to transmit a signal which can be picked up by the radar on a rescue vessel so they can find you.

Helicopter rescue

If a helicopter has to be scrambled to assist you, there are certain procedures that all crew need to know and preparations to make:

* Lower and stow all sails and any obstructions and make fast any loose rigging.
* Stow any loose items that are on deck that may obstruct the lift or get blown about by the rotors.
* If a casualty is to be airlifted, get them up on deck, dressed in warm clothing if possible.
* If the whole crew need to abandon the boat, make sure they are wearing warm clothing and lifejackets and get the liferaft ready in case of delay in rescue. Don't try to take any items except small pocket-sized valuables.

Communications

Contact the helicopter pilot as soon as possible on VHF. He will need to know as much detail as possible regarding number of casualties/persons to lift, wind direction, state of the boat if in danger of sinking.

Have a handheld smoke flare (not a rocket flare) ready to help the pilot to identify you.

When the helicopter arrives

Don't shine strong lights at the helicopter at night.

Don't touch the winchman, stretcher, or hi-line until static electricity has been discharged on the deck or in the water.

Don't attach anything from the helicopter to the boat.

Don't use the radio when the winching is happening unless it is very urgent. The winchman will probably use hand signals to communicate with you.

A crewmember will probably be asked to look after the hi-line: if the pick up is aft then guide the line into the cockpit; if it is on the foredeck, stow the lose end in a bucket. **Do not attach it to the boat**. The helicopter pilot will give instructions as to how to handle the line. If there is no radio contact, then, wearing gloves, you pull the line in (after it has been earthed) and steady it as the winchman is lowered to deck level.

A Coastguard helicopter carrying out a practice lift from a motor boat.

SAILING QUIZ

Parts of the boat

1 Fill in these positions on the drawing:
  a Bow
  b Stern
  c Port side
  d Starboard side

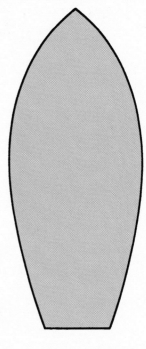

2 Look at the drawing above. In relation to the boat, what positions are the following:
  ◆ The powerboat
  ◆ The rowing boat
  ◆ The buoy

3 Name the parts of the boat on these drawings:
  a Fore hatch
  b Main hatch
  c Cockpit
  d Mast
  e Boom
  f Pulpit
  g Pushpit
  h Guardrail
  i Stanchion
  j Keel
  k Rudder
  l Tiller

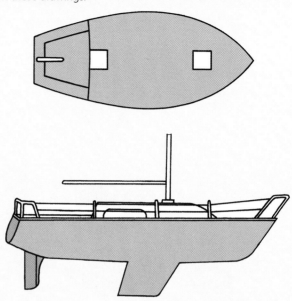

4 Name the parts of the sail marked a-f

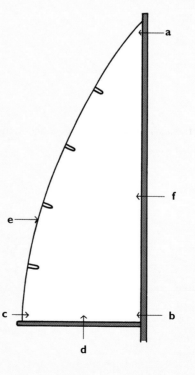

5 Fill in which point of sailing the boats are on and which tack.

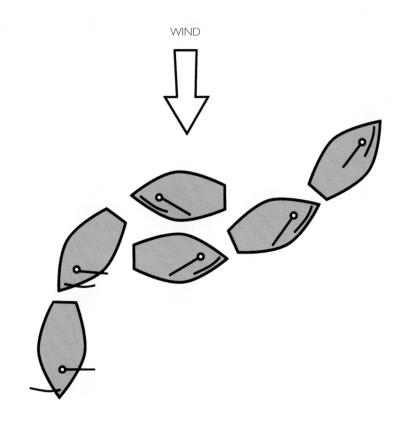

6 What are the lines a, b, c and d called? What do they do?

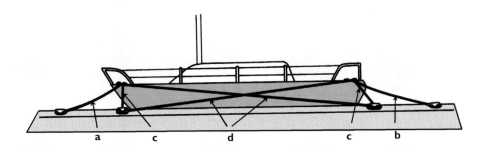

7   What tack is this boat on?

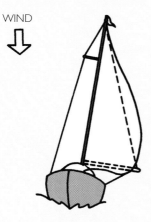

8   Show the positions of the sails and the rudder when the boat is hove-to:

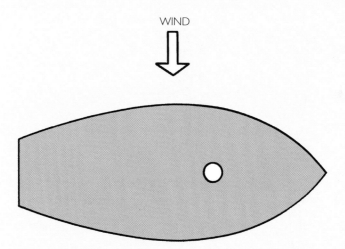

9 What are the parts of the rope called?

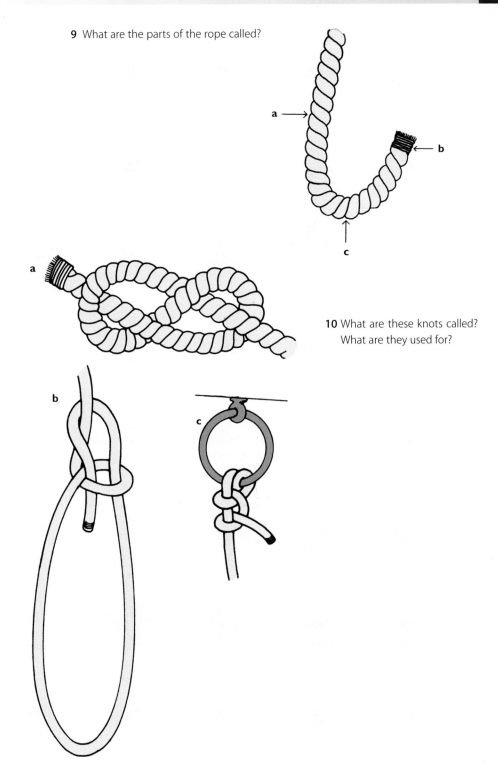

10 What are these knots called?
What are they used for?

11 What is this anchor called?

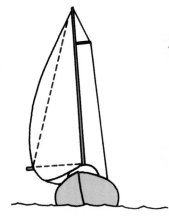

12 This boat is sailing with a full mainsail and a large genoa. A gale has been forecast. If she stays on the same course and the wind increases to force 8, what sails should she be carrying?

13 The navigator on this boat is taking a compass bearing of the lighthouse and the radio mast when they are in transit. The bearing is 356°C. The true bearing given on the chart is 358°T and variation is 6°W. What is the deviation?

14 Name the cardinal buoys in this drawing:

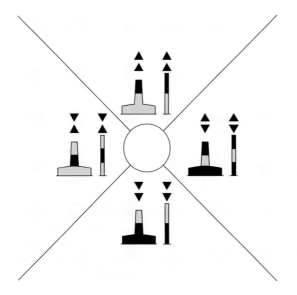

15 If you are entering harbour and see these buoys, what is their significance to you?

16 What do these buoys indicate?

a   b

17 This sailing boat is approaching a cardinal mark. To which side of the boat should she leave the buoy?

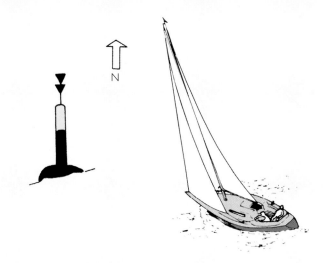

18 Your yacht has just anchored. How can you tell if her anchor is dragging?

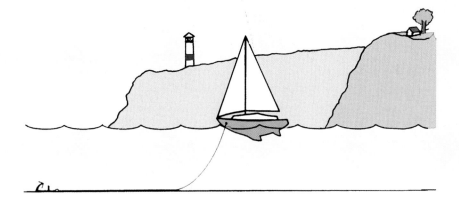

19 When sailing or motoring along a channel, how can this skipper use shore marks to navigate safely?

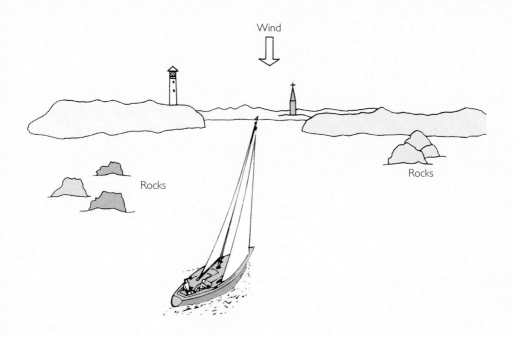

20 What are the tree branches stuck in the river mud called? What are they for?

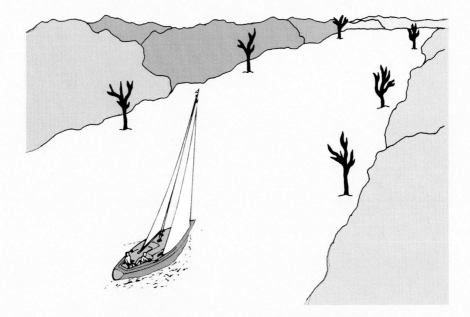

21 How can the power boat tell if she is on a collision course with the sailing boat?

22 These two boats are both under power. Which one has the right of way (is the stand-on vessel)?

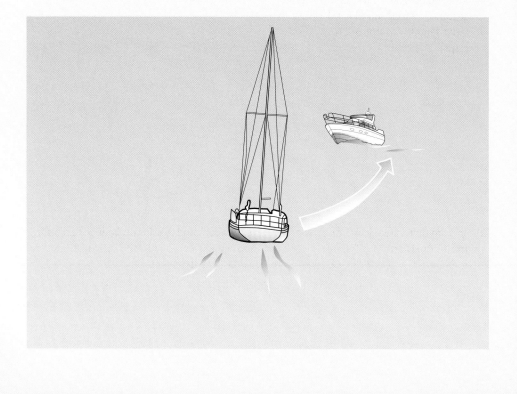

23 The sailing boat is overtaking the fishing boat. Who has the right of way?

24 What colours are shown on the four sectors of this all round light? Up to what length of boat is allowed to display this light?

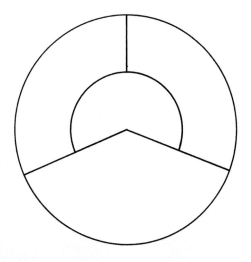

25 You are on a catamaran *Scaredy Cat*; you have hit a rock and are sinking. Your position is five miles from Land's End. The bearing of Land's end from Scaredy Cat is 060°T. There are six crew members on board including yourself. What VHF call would you make?

ANSWERS TO THE QUIZ

1

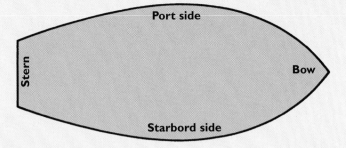

2 ◆ The powerboat is ahead
  ◆ The rowing boat is abeam to port
  ◆ The buoy is astern

3 Parts of the boat

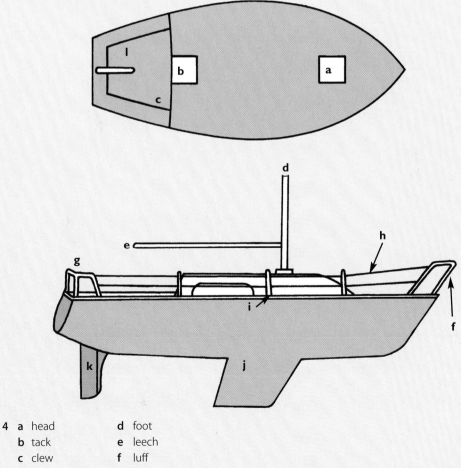

4 **a** head   **d** foot
   b tack   **e** leech
   c clew   **f** luff

5 Points of sailing

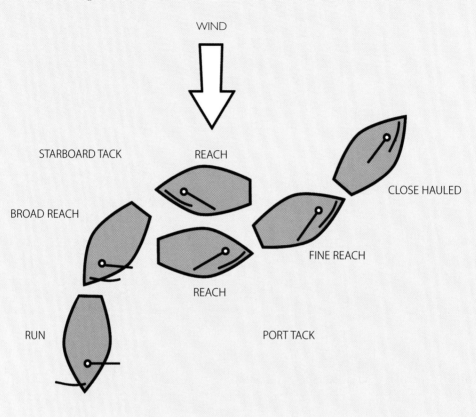

WIND

STARBOARD TACK   REACH

CLOSE HAULED

BROAD REACH

FINE REACH

REACH

RUN   PORT TACK

6 **a** bow line
   b stern line
   c breast lines
   d springs

♦ The bow and stern lines hold the boat's bows and stern in.
♦ The breast lines keep the boat alongside.
♦ The springs stop the boat moving fore and aft.

7 This boat is on starboard tack.

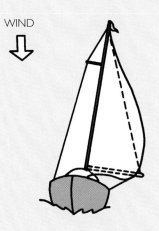

8 Positions of sails and rudder when the boat is hove-to.

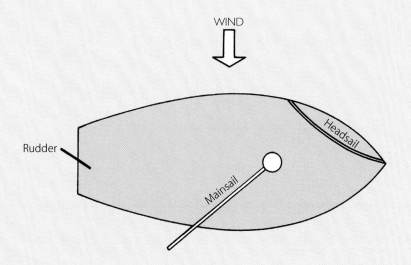

9 **a** standing part
   b bight
   c end

10 **a** stopper knot or figure of eight
   b bowline
   c round turn and two half hitches

   a to stop the end of a sheet pulling through a block
   b to put a temporary eye in a rope
   c for securing a mooring line to a ring

11 CQR – holds well in soft sand and mud.

12 She would be probably running before the wind with a storm jib only.

13 Deviation 8°E.

14 Cardinal buoys.

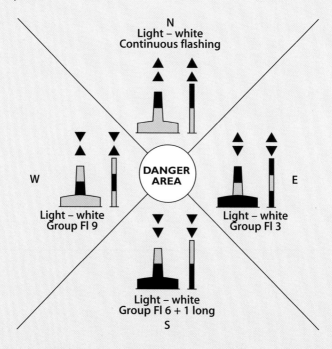

15 The buoy on the left indicates that the preferred channel is to starboard. The one on the right gives the preferred channel to port.

16 a an isolated danger mark which is placed over an obstruction
b a safe water mark which indicates safe water all round it

17 To starboard.

18 By taking bearings of shore objects at regular intervals.

19 He or she can use clearing bearings from the lighthouse and the church to stay in safe water away from the rocks.

20 Withies. They are used to mark a safe channel.

21 By taking a compass bearing at regular intervals. If the bearing does not alter, the boats are on a collision course.

22 The motorboat has right of way.

23 The fishing boat has right of way as it is the boat which is being overtaken.

24 Boats up to 20m can carry this light.

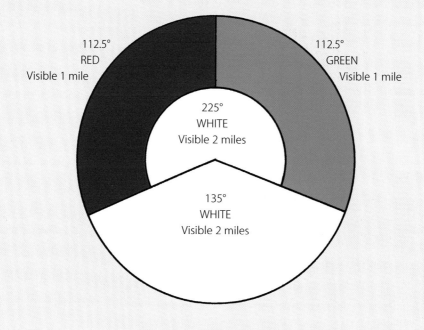

112.5°
RED
Visible 1 mile

112.5°
GREEN
Visible 1 mile

225°
WHITE
Visible 2 miles

135°
WHITE
Visible 2 miles

25 Mayday, Mayday, Mayday
This is yacht Scaredy Cat, Yacht Scaredy Cat, Yacht Scaredy Cat
Mayday Yacht Scaredy Cat
My position is two four zero Land's End five miles
I am sinking and require immediate assistance
I have six persons on board
Over

appendix 1 – course syllabus

Royal Yachting Association
Competent Crew Practical Course Syllabus

Aim: To introduce the complete beginner to cruising and to teach personal safety, seamanship and helmsmanship to the level required to be a useful member of the crew of a cruising yacht.

1 **Knowledge of sea terms and parts of a boat, her rigging and sails**
   Sufficient knowledge to understand orders given concerning the sailing and day-to-day running of the boat.

2 **Sail handling**
   Bending on, setting, reefing and handling of sails. Use of sheets and halyards and their associated winches.

3 **Ropework**
   Handling ropes, including coiling, stowing, securing to cleats and single and double bollards. Handling warps. Ability to tie the following knots and to know their correct use: figure of eight, clove hitch, rolling hitch, bowline, round turn and two half hitches, single and double sheet bend, reef knot.

4 **Fire precautions and fighting**
   Awareness of the hazards of fire, the precautions necessary to prevent fire and the action to be taken in event of fire.

5 **Personal safety equipment**
   Understands and complies with rules for the wearing of safety harnesses, lifejackets and personal buoyancy aids.

6 **Man overboard**
   Understands action to be taken to recover a man overboard.

7 **Distress signals**
   Can operate distress flares and knows on what occasions distress flares should be used.

8 Manners and customs

Understands the ordinary practice of seamen and yachtsmen with regard to: use of burgees and ensigns, prevention of unnecessary noise or disturbance in harbour, including courtesies to other craft berthed alongside.

9 Rules of the road

Is able to keep an efficient lookout at sea.

10 Dinghies

Understands and complies with the loading rules. Is able to handle a dinghy under oars.

11 Meteorology

Awareness of forecasting services and knowledge of the Beaufort scale.

12 Seasickness

Working efficiency unaffected/partially affected/severely affected by seasickness.

13 Helmsmanship and sailing

Understands the theory of sailing and can steer and trim sails on all points of sailing. Can steer a compass course, under sail and power.

appendix 2 – glossary

Aback A sail is aback when the wind strikes it on what would normally be its lee side.

Abaft the beam The sector on both sides of a boat from abeam to astern.

Abeam The direction at right angles to the fore-and-aft line.

Aft Near or towards the stern.

Ahead The direction of an object beyond the stem of a boat.

Ahoy Shout this to attract attention of another vessel.

Alee To leeward.

Almanac An annual publication containing information on, for example, buoyage, tides, signals, glossaries, and positions of heavenly bodies.

Aloft Above deck.

Amidships The centre part of the boat.

Anchor buoy Buoy or float secured by a tripping line to the crown of the anchor.

Anchor cable Chain or rope connection between a boat and her anchor.

Anchor light An all round white light usually shackled to the forestay of a boat and hoisted to a suitable height by the jib halyard.

Anchor locker A locker for the anchor and anchor chain.

Anchor roller A roller over which the anchor cable is passed when at anchor.

Anchor watch Watch kept when a boat is at anchor to check whether the anchor is dragging.

Anchor well See *anchor locker*.

Answer the helm A boat answers the helm when she alters course in response to the helmsman's deflection of the rudder.

Apparent wind The wind felt by the crew in a boat that is moving over the ground.

Ashore On the land; or aground.

Astern Direction beyond the stern; or a movement through the water in that direction.

Athwartships At right angles to the centreline of the boat inside the boat.

Autopilot equipment that allows the boat to follow automatically a compass course or a course relative to wind direction.

Auxiliary A term for a sailing boat that has auxiliary power, ie an engine.

Avast Order to stop an activity.

Awash Level with the surface of the water which just washes over an object.

Babystay An inner forestay.

Back To back a sail: it is sheeted or held to windward so that the wind strikes it on the side which is normally to leeward. Of wind: it backs when it shifts to blow from a direction that is further anticlockwise.

Back splice The end of a rope that has been finished by unlaying the strands, making a crown knot and tucking the strands back down the rope.

Backstay A stay which supports the mast from aft.

Backwind Airflow that is deflected on to the lee side of a sail, such as a jib backwinding the mainsail.

Bail To remove water from the bilges or cockpit.

Bailer A utensil used to bail water out of a boat.

Ball A black signal shape normally displayed by day when a boat is at anchor.

Ballast Additional weight placed low in the hull to improve stability.

Bar A shoal close by a river mouth or harbour entrance; a measure of barometric pressure usually noted as 1000 millibars.

Bare poles No sails are set and the boat is driven by the force of the wind on the spars and rigging.

Barnacle A marine crustacean that attaches itself to the bottom of a boat.

Batten A flexible strip of wood or plastic used to stiffen the leech of a sail.

Batten pocket A pocket on the leech of a sail to contain a batten.

Beach To run a boat ashore deliberately.

Beacon A mark erected on land or on the bottom in shallow waters to guide or warn shipping.

Beam The breadth of a boat.

Beam reach A point of sailing with the wind roughly at right angles to the fore-and-aft line.

Bear away To put the helm to windward so that the boat alters course to leeward away from the wind.

Bearing The direction of an object from an observer given as an angle from a line of reference (true north or magnetic north).

Bearings (3-figure notation) Bearings and courses are given in a 3-figure notation, that is: 180°C or 180°T depending on whether it is a Compass or True bearing.

Beating Sailing towards an objective to windward following a zigzag course on alternate tacks.

Beaufort scale A scale for measurement of the force of the wind.

Belay To make fast a line round a cleat or bollard.

Bell In restricted visibility a bell is rung to indicate that a boat is at anchor or aground.

Below deck Beneath the deck.

Bend To connect two ropes with a knot; to prepare a sail for hoisting; a type of knot.

Berth A place where a boat can lie for a period; a sleeping place on a boat (see bunk); to give an obstruction a wide berth by keeping well clear.

Bight A loop or curve in a rope or line.

Bilge The rounded part of a boat where the bottom curves upwards towards the sides.

Bilges The lowest part inside the hull below the cabin sole where bilge water collects.

Bilge keel One of two keels fitted on either side of a boat's hull to resist rolling and provide lateral resistance.

Binnacle Strong housing to protect the steering compass.

Blanket To take the wind from another boat's sails.

Blast (foghorn) A sound signal – a short blast lasts 1 second, a prolonged blast 4 to 6 seconds.

Block A pulley made of wood, metal or plastic.

Boathook A pole, generally of wood or light alloy, with a hook at one end, used for picking up moorings and buoys.

Bollard Strong fitting, firmly bolted to the deck, to which mooring lines are made fast. Large bollards are on quays, piers and pontoons.

Bolt rope Rope sewn to one or more edges of a sail either to reinforce the sides or so that the sail can be fed into a grooved spar.

Boom Spar that supports the foot of the sail.

Boom out On a run to thrust the genoa out to windward with a whisker pole so that it fills with wind.

Boot top A narrow stripe just above the waterline between the bottom and side of the hull. Usually of contrasting colour.

Bottlescrew A rigging screw to tension the standing rigging or guardrails.

Bow The forward part of a boat. A direction 45° either side of right ahead.

Bowline A knot tied in the end of a line to make a loop that will neither slip nor jam.

Breakwater A structure built to protect a harbour or beach from the force of the sea.

Breast rope A mooring line that runs at right angles to the centreline; one runs from the bow, another from the stern to the shore or a boat alongside.

Broach With heavy following seas the boat can slew round uncontrollably, heeling dangerously.

Breather A pipe fitted to a water or fuel tank which allows air to escape.

Broad reach The point of sailing between a beam reach and a run.

Broken out The anchor, when pulled out of the seabed by heaving on the cable, is broken out.

Bulkhead A vertical partition below decks.

Bunk A built-in sleeping place.

Buoy A floating object used to indicate the position of a channel, wreck, danger, etc, or the position of an object on the seabed.

Buoyancy aid A life-preserver to help a person float if he falls in; less effective than a lifejacket.

Burgee A triangular flag worn at the masthead.

Cabin The sheltered area in which the crew live and sleep.

Cable Chain or rope that is made fast to the anchor. A measure of distance equivalent to one tenth of a nautical mile.

Capsize The boat overturns.

Cast off To let go a rope or line.

Cavita line A decorative line of contrasting colour on the hull of the boat, near the rubbing strake.

Centreboard A board lowered through a slot in the keel to reduce leeway by providing lateral resistance.

Chafe Damage or wear resulting from friction.

Chain locker See *anchor locker*.

Chainplate A fitting which is bolted to the hull, to which the shrouds are attached.

Chandler A shop which sells nautical gear.

Channel A waterway through shoals, rivers or harbours.

Chart Printed map giving many details about the area covered by water and details about the adjacent land.

Chart datum Reference level on charts and for use in tidal predictions.

Clear To disentangle a line; to avoid a danger or obstruction; improved weather.

Cleat A fitting with two horns round which a rope is secured.

Clevis pin A locking pin with an eye at one end through which a split ring is fitted to prevent accidental withdrawal.

Clew The after lower corner of a sail to which the sheets are fitted.

Clew outhaul The line which tensions the foot of the mainsail.

Close hauled The point of sailing when the boat is as close to the wind as she can lie with advantage in working to windward.

Coachroof The part of the cabin that is raised above the deck to provide height in the cabin.

Coaming Vertical structure surrounding a hatch or cockpit to prevent water entering.

Coast radio station A radio station for communication between ships at sea and the public telephone network.

Coastguard The organisation responsible for search and rescue operations in UK waters.

Cocked hat In navigation the triangle formed when three position lines fail to meet at a single point.

Cockpit A space lower than deck level in which the crew can sit or stand.

Collision course The course of a boat which, if maintained relative to that of another, would result in a collision.

Compass rose A circle printed on a chart representing the true compass and graduated clockwise from 0° to 360°.

Cone A signal shape displayed either point upwards or point downwards.

Counter Above the waterline where the stern extends beyond the rudder post forming a broad afterdeck abaft the cockpit.

Course The direction in which the boat is being, or is to be, steered.

Courtesy ensign The national flag of the country being visited by a foreign boat; it should be flown from the starboard spreader.

CQR anchor A patented anchor with good holding power.

Cringle A rope loop, usually with a metal thimble, worked in the edge of a sail.

Crutch see *Rowlock*. Also a support for the boom when the mainsail is lowered.

Dan buoy A temporary mark to indicate a position, say, of a man overboard. A flag flies from a spar passing through a float and weighted at the bottom.

Deck log A book in which all details concerning navigation are entered or logged.

Depth sounder See *Echo sounder*.

Deviation The deflection of the needle of a magnetic compass caused by the proximity of ferrous metals, electrical circuits or electronic equipment.

Dip the ensign To lower the ensign briefly as a salute. It is not rehoisted until the vessel saluted has dipped and rehoisted hers in acknowledgement.

Displacement The weight of a boat defined as the weight of water displaced by that boat.

Distance made good The distance covered over the ground having made allowance for tidal stream and leeway.

Dividers Navigational instrument for measuring distances on charts.

Dodger Screen fitted to give the crew protection from wind and spray.

Dolphin A mooring post or group of piles.

Double up To put out extra mooring lines when a storm is expected.

Douse To lower a sail or extinguish a light quickly.

Downhaul A rope or line with which a spar or sail is pulled down.

Downwind Direction to leeward.

Downstream The direction towards which the stream flows.

Drag The anchor drags when it fails to hold and slides over the sea-bed.

Draught The vertical distance from the lowest part of the keel to the waterline.

Dress ship On special occasions ships in harbour or at anchor dress overall with International Code flags from the stem to the mast head and down to the stern.

Drift To be carried by the tidal stream. The distance that a boat is carried by the tidal stream in a given time.

Drop astern To fall astern of another boat.

Drop keel A keel that can be drawn up into the hull.

Ease out To slacken a rope gradually.

Ebb The period when the tidal level is falling.

Echo sounder An electronic depth-finding instrument.

Ensign The national flag worn at or near the stern of a boat to indicate her nationality.

EPIRB An Emergency Position Indicating Radio Beacon that transmits a distinctive signal on a distress frequency.

Even keel A boat floating so that her mast is more or less vertically upright.

Eye A loop or eye splice. The eyes of a boat: right forward.

Eyelet A small hole in a sail with a metal grommet through which lacing is passed.

Eye splice A permanent eye spliced in the end of a rope or wire rope.

Fair Advantageous or favourable, as of wind or tide.

Fairlead The lead through which a working line is passed in order to alter the direction of pull.

Fairway The main channel in a body of water such as an estuary or river.

Fender Any device hung outboard to absorb the shock when coming alongside and to protect the hull when moored alongside.

Fetch The distance travelled by the wind when crossing open water: the height of the waves is proportional to the fetch and strength of the wind.

Fin keel A short keel bolted to the hull.

Fix The position of a boat as plotted on the chart from position lines obtained by compass bearings, direction finder, echo sounder, etc.

Flake down Rope laid down on deck in a figure of eight pattern so that it will run out easily.

Flashing A light used as an aid to navigation that flashes repeatedly at regular intervals where the dark period exceeds the light period.

Flood The period when the tidal level is rising.

Fluke The shovel-shaped part of an anchor that digs into the ground.

Flying out A sail is flying out in a breeze when it has no tension in the sheets.

Focsle The part of the accommodation below the foredeck and forward of the mast.

Fog Visibility reduced to less than 1000 metres (approx. 0.5 nautical miles).

Following sea Seas that are moving in the same direction as the boat is heading.

Foot The lower edge of a sail.

Fore-and-aft Parallel to the line between the stem and the stern.

Foredeck The part of the deck that is forward of the mast and coachroof.

Forefoot The area below the water where the stem joins the keel.

Forehatch A hatch forward, usually in the foredeck.

Forepeak The most forward compartment in the bows of the boat.

Foresail The headsail set on the forestay.

Forestay The stay from high on the mast to the stemhead providing fore-and-aft support for the mast.

Foul The opposite of clear; adverse (wind or tide); unsuitable.

Foul anchor An anchor whose flukes are caught on an obstruction on the sea-bed or tangled with the cable.

Frap Tie halyards to keep them off the mast to stop them rattling noisily in the wind when in harbour.

Freeboard The vertical distance between the waterline and the top of the deck.

Free wind The wind when it blows from a direction abaft the beam.

Front (air mass) Boundary between air masses at different temperatures.

Full and by Close-hauled with all sails full and drawing; not pinching.

Full rudder The maximum angle to which the rudder can be turned.

Furling Rolling up or gathering and lashing a lowered sail using sail ties or shockcord to prevent it from blowing about.

Gale In the Beaufort scale, wind force 8, 34 to 40 knots. Severe gale, force 9, is 41 to 47 knots.

Galley An area where food is prepared and cooked.

Gelcoat The outer unreinforced layer of resin in a Glass Reinforced Plastic (GRP) hull.

Genoa A large overlapping headsail set in light to fresh winds.

Ghoster A light full headsail set in light breezes.

Give-way vessel The vessel whose duty it is to keep clear of another; she should take early and substantial action to avoid a collision.

Go about To change from one tack to another by luffing and turning the bows through the wind.

Gong A fog signal sounded in conjunction with a bell in a vessel over 100m in length when at anchor or aground.

Gooseneck Fitting which attaches the boom to the mast.

Goosewing To fly the headsail on the opposite side to the mainsail (using a spinnaker pole or whisker pole perhaps) when running.

GPS Global Positioning System – electronic satellite navigation.

Grab rail Rails fitted above and below decks to hold on to when the boat heels.

Ground To run aground or touch the bottom either accidentally or deliberately.

Ground tackle A general term for the anchors, cables and all the gear required when anchoring.

Groyne See *Breakwater*.

GRP Glass Reinforced Plastic.

Guardrail Safety line fitted round the boat to prevent the crew from falling overboard.

Gunwale The upper edge of the side of a boat.

Guy A line attached to the end of a spar to keep it in position.

Gybe To change from one tack to another by turning the stern through the wind.

Gybe-oh The warning given when the helm is put across to gybe.

Hail To shout loudly to crew in another boat.

Half hitch A simple knot.

Halyard A line or rope with which a sail, spar or flag is hoisted up a mast.

Hand-bearing compass Portable magnetic compass with which visual bearings are taken.

Handrail A wooden or metal rail on the coachroof or below deck which can be grasped to steady a person.

Hanks Fittings made of metal or nylon by which the luff of a staysail is held to a stay.

Hard Hard ground where boats can be launched.

Hard and fast Said of a boat that has run aground and is unable to get off immediately.

Harden in To haul in the sheets to bring the sail closer to the centreline; the opposite of ease out.

Hatch An opening in the deck that allows access to the accommodation.

Haul in To pull in.

Hawse pipe A hole in the bow of a vessel through which the anchor cable passes.

Haze Visibility reduced to between 1,000 and 2,000 metres (0.5 to 1 nautical mile) by dry particles in suspension in the air.

Head The bow or forward part of the boat. The upper corner of a triangular sail.

Head line The mooring line or rope leading forward from the bows.

Head to wind To point the stem of the boat into the wind.

Heading The direction in which the boat's head is pointing, her course.

Headland A fairly high and steep part of the land that projects into the sea.

Heads The lavatory on a boat.

Headsail Any sail set forward of the mast or of the foremast if there is more than one mast.

Headway Movement through the water stem first.

Heaving line A light line coiled ready for throwing; sometimes the end is weighted.

Heaving-to A boat heaves-to when she goes about leaving the headsail sheeted on the original side so it is backed. Ideal manoeuvre for reefing in heavy weather.

Heel To lean over to one side.

Height of tide The vertical distance at any instant between sea level and chart datum.

Helmsman The member of the crew who steers the boat.

Hitch A type of knot.

Hoist To raise an object vertically with a halyard.

Holding ground The composition of the sea-bed that determines whether the anchor will hold well or not.

Hull The body of a boat excluding masts, rigging and rudder.

Hull down Said of a distant vessel when only the mast, sails and/or superstructure is visible above the horizon.

Hydrofoil A boat with hydrofoils that lift the wetted surface of her hull clear of the water at speed.

Hydrography The science of surveying the waters of the earth and adjacent land areas and publishing the results in charts, pilots, etc.

IALA The International Association of Lighthouse Authorities which is responsible for the international buoyage system.

Impeller Screw-like device which is rotated by water flowing past: used for measuring boat speed and distance travelled through the water.

In irons Said of a boat that stops head to wind when going about.

Inshore Near to or towards or in the direction of the shore.

Isobar On a synoptic chart, a line joining points of equal pressure.

Isophase A light where the duration of light and dark are equal.

Jackstay A wire secured between two points.

Jam cleat (self-jamming) A cleat with one horn shorter than the other designed so that a rope can be secured with a single turn.

Jib Triangular headsail set on a stay forward of the mast.

Jury rig A temporary but effective device that replaces lost or damaged gear.

Kedge anchor A lightweight anchor used to move a boat or to anchor temporarily in fine weather.

Keel The main longitudinal beam on a boat between the stem and the stern.

Ketch A two-masted boat where the after (mizzen) mast is smaller and is stepped forward of the rudder stock.

kHz (kilohertz) A measurement of frequency of radio waves equivalent to 1,000 cycles per second.

Kicking strap Line or tackle to pull the boom down in order to keep it horizontal.

Kink A sharp twist in a rope or wire rope; can be avoided by coiling the rope properly.

Knot The unit of speed at sea; one nautical mile per hour; a series of loops in rope or line.

Landfall Land first sighted after a long voyage at sea.

Lanyard A short length of line used to secure an object such as a knife.

Lash down To secure firmly with rope or line.

Lay Strands twisted together to form a rope. To lay a mark is to sail directly to it without tacking.

Lead line A line marked with knots at regular intervals and attached to a heavy weight to determine the depth of water.

Lee The direction towards which the wind blows.

Leeboard A board or strip of canvas along the open side of a berth to prevent the occupant from falling out.

Lee helm The tendency of a boat to turn her bow to leeward.

Lee-oh The warning given when the helm is put across to go about.

Leech The trailing edge of a triangular or quadrilateral sail.

Lee shore A coastline towards which the onshore wind blows; the shore to leeward of a boat.

Leeward Downwind, away from the wind, the direction towards which the wind blows.

Leeward boat When two boats are on the same tack, the leeward boat is that which is to leeward of the other.

Leeway The angular difference between the water track and the boat's heading. The effect of wind moving the boat bodily to leeward.

Lifeline A wire or line attached at either end to a strong point and rigged along the deck as a handhold or for clipping on a safety harness.

Line Alternative name for small size rope or for a rope used for mooring a boat.

Line of soundings Numerous soundings taken at regular intervals.

List A permanent lean to one side or the other.

List of lights Official publication giving details of lights exhibited as aids to navigation.

LOA Length overall.

Loafer A lightweight sail used when reaching or running in light winds.

Lock A chamber in a navigation with gates at each end in which the water level can be raised or lowered.

Locker An enclosed stowage anywhere on board.

Locking turns A reversed turn on a cleat to make a rope more secure; not advisable for halyards which may need to be cast off quickly.

Log A device to measure a boat's speed or distance travelled through the water. See *Deck Log*.

Log reading The reading of distance travelled through the water usually taken every hour from the log and recorded in the deck log.

Look-out Visual watch; or the member of the crew responsible for keeping a visual watch.

Loom The glow from a light below the horizon usually seen as a reflection on the clouds.

Lop Short choppy seas.

Lose way A boat loses way when she slows down and stops in the water.

Lubber line The marker in the compass which is aligned with the fore-and-aft line of the boat against which the course can be read off on the compass card.

Luff The leading edge of a fore-and-aft sail.

Lull A temporary drop in wind speed.

Mainsail The principal sail.

Mainsheet traveller The athwartships slider to which the mainsheet tackle is made fast.

Make fast To secure a line or rope to a cleat, mooring ring, bollard, etc.

Make sail To hoist the sails and get under way.

Make water To leak but not by shipping water over the side.

Marina Artificial boat harbour usually consisting of pontoons.

Mark An object that marks a position.

Maroon An explosive signal used to summon the crew when a lifeboat is called out.

Mast The most important vertical spar without which no sail can be set.

Mast step Fitting into which the mast heel fits.

Masthead light A white light exhibited near the masthead by a power-driven vessel under way.

Masthead rig A boat with the forestay attached to the masthead.

Mayday The internationally recognised radio telephone distress signal.

Medico When included in an urgency call (Pan Pan) on the radio telephone, Medico indicates that medical advice is required.

MHWS (Mean High Water Springs) The average level of all high water heights at spring tides throughout the year: used as the datum level for heights of features on the chart.

Mist Visibility reduced to between 1,000 and 2,000 metres (0.5 to 1 nautical miles) due to the suspension of water particles in the air.

Mizzen mast The smaller aftermast of a ketch or yawl.

Mole A breakwater made of stone or concrete.

Monohull A boat with a single hull.

Mooring The ground tackle attached to a mooring buoy.

Mooring buoy A non-navigational buoy to which a boat can moor.

Mooring ring A ring on a mooring pile to which head and stern lines are secured.

Multihull A boat with more than one hull such as a catamaran or trimaran.

Nautical mile Unit of distance at sea based on the length of one minute of latitude.

Navel pipe A pipe which passes through the deck to the anchor chain locker.

Navigation lights Lights exhibited by all vessels between sunset and sunrise.

Neap tide Tides where the range is least and the tidal streams run least strongly.

No-sail sector An area either side of the wind, in which a boat cannot sail.

Nominal range of a light Nominal range of a light is dependent on its intensity: it is the luminous range when the meteorological visibility is 10 nautical miles.

Not under command A vessel unable to manoeuvre such as one whose rudder has been damaged.

Notices to mariners Official notices issued weekly or at other times detailing corrections to charts and hydrographic publications.

Null The bearing of a radio beacon at which the signal tends to disappear when the aerial of a direction finder is rotated.

Occulting light A rhythmic light eclipsing at regular intervals so that the duration of light in each period is greater than the duration of darkness.

Offing The part of the sea that is visible from the shore. To keep an offing is to keep a safe distance from the shore.

Oilskins Waterproof clothing worn in foul weather.

On the bow A direction about 45° from right ahead on either side of the boat.

On the quarter A direction about 45° from right astern on either side of the boat.

Open When two leading marks are not in line they are said to be open.

Osmosis Water absorption through tiny pinholes in a GRP hull causing deterioration of the moulding.

Outhaul A line with which the mainsail clew is hauled out along the boom.

Overcanvassed A boat carrying too much sail for the weather conditions.

Overfalls Turbulent water where there is a sudden change in depth or where two tidal streams meet.

Overtaking light The white stern light; seen by an overtaking vessel when approaching from astern.

Painter The line at the bow of a dinghy.

Pan pan The internationally recognised radio telephone urgency signal which has priority over all other calls except Mayday.

Parallel rules Navigational instrument used in conjunction with the compass rose on a chart to transfer bearings and courses to plot a boat's position.

Pay off The boat's head pays off when it turns to leeward away from the wind.

Pay out To let out a line or rope gradually.

Period Of a light, the time that it takes a rhythmic light to complete one sequence.

Pile A stout timber, concrete or metal post driven vertically into a river or seabed.

Pilot An expert in local waters who assists vessels entering or leaving harbour. An official publication listing details of, for example, local coasts, dangers and harbours.

Pilot berth A berth or bunk for use at sea.

Pinch To sail too close to the wind so that the sails lose driving power.

Pipe cot A spare berth on a pipe frame that hinges up when not in use.

Piston hanks A hank on the luff of a staysail.

Pitch The up and down motion of the bow and stern of a boat.

Pitchpole A capsize in a following sea where the stern is lifted over the bow.

Play To adjust a sheet continuously rather than cleating it. Movement of equipment such as the rudder in its mounting or housing.

Plot To find a boat's position by laying off bearings on a chart.

Plotter A tool incorporating a compass rose which can be swivelled.

Plough anchor An anchor shaped like a ploughshare similar to a CQR anchor.

Point The ability of a boat to sail close hauled: the closer she sails the better she points. A division of 11° 15′ on the compass.

Poling out Using a spar to push a foresail out when running.

Pontoon A watertight tank, usually between piles, that rises and falls with the tide often with planks on top to provide a mooring.

Pooped A boat in a situation when a following sea has broken over the stern into the cockpit.

Port hand A direction on the port or left-hand side of a boat.

Port side The left-hand side of a boat when looking towards the bow.

Position line A line drawn on a chart by the navigator.

Pound A boat pounds in heavy seas when the bows drop heavily after being lifted by a wave.

Prevailing wind The wind direction that occurs most frequently at a particular place over a certain period.

Preventer A line rigged from the end of the boom to the bow in heavy weather to prevent an accidental gybe.

Privileged vessel The stand-on vessel in a collision situation: she should maintain her course and speed.

Pull To row.

Pulpit Stainless steel frame at the bow encircling the forestay to which the guardrails are attached.

Pushpit Colloquial term for the stern pulpit.

Pyrotechnic Any type of rocket or flare used for signalling. Red pyrotechnics indicate distress.

Quarter Either side of the hull between amidships and astern.
Quarter berth A berth that extends under the side deck between the cockpit and the hull.

Race A strong tidal stream.
Radar reflector A device hoisted or fitted up the mast to enhance the reflection of radar energy.
Raft of boats Two or more boats tied up alongside each other.
Range of tide The difference between sea level at high water and sea level at the preceding or following low water.
Rate The speed of a tidal stream or current given in knots and tenths of a knot.
Reach A boat is on a reach when she is neither close-hauled or running. It is her fastest point of sail.
Ready about The helmsman's shout that he intends to go about shortly.
Reciprocal course The course (or bearing) that differs from another course by 180°.
Reef To reduce the area of sail, particularly the mainsail.
Reef points Short light lines sewn into the sail parallel with the boom that are tied under the foot (or the boom itself) when the sail is reefed.
Reefing pennants A strong line with which the luff and leech are pulled down to the boom when a sail is reefed.
Relative bearing The direction of an object relative to the fore-and-aft line of a boat measured in degrees from right ahead.
Relative wind See *Apparent wind*.
Restricted visibility Visibility restricted by rain, drizzle, fog, etc., during which vessels are required to proceed at a safe speed and to navigate with extreme caution.
Rhumb line A line on the surface of the earth that cuts all meridians at the same angle. On a standard (Mercator) chart the rhumb line appears as a straight line.
Ride To lie at anchor free to swing to the wind and tidal stream.
Ridge On a synoptic chart, a narrow area of relatively high pressure between two low pressure areas.
Riding light Alternative term for anchor light.
Riding turn On a winch the situation where an earlier turn rides over a later turn and jams.
Rigging All ropes, lines, wires and gear used to support the masts and to control the spars and sails.
Right of way Term used for the vessel which does not give way.
Risk of collision A possibility that a collision may occur; usually established by taking a compass bearing of an approaching vessel.
Roads An anchorage where the holding ground is known to be good and there is some protection from the wind and sea.
Roll The periodic rotating movement of a boat that leans alternately to port and starboard.
Roller reef A method of reefing where the sail area is reduced by rolling part of the sail around the boom.
Rolling hitch A knot used to attach a small line to a larger line or spar.
Round To sail around a mark.
Round turn A complete turn of a rope or line around an object. The rope completely encircles the object.
Round up To head up into the wind.
Roving fender A spare fender held ready by a crew member for use in case of emergencies.
Rowlock A U-shaped fitting which supplies a fulcrum for the oar.
Rubbing strake A projecting strake round the top of a hull to protect the hull when lying alongside.

Rudder A control surface in the water at or near the stern, used for altering course.

Run The point of sailing where a boat sails in the same direction as the wind is blowing with her sheets eased right out.

Run down To collide with another boat.

Runner A backstay that supports the mast from aft and can be slacked off.

Running fix A navigational fix when only a single landmark is available. Two bearings are taken and plotted at different times making allowance for distance travelled.

Running rigging All rigging that moves and is not part of the standing rigging.

Sacrificial anode A zinc plate fastened to the hull to prevent corrosion of metal fittings on the hull.

Sail locker Place where sails are stowed.

Sail ties Light lines used to lash a lowered sail to the boom or guardrails to prevent it blowing about.

Sailing directions Also called Pilot books. Official publications covering specific areas containing navigational information concerning, for example, coasts, harbours and tides.

Sailing free Not close hauled; sailing with sheets eased out.

Saloon The main cabin.

Salvage The act of saving a vessel from danger at sea.

Samson post Strong fitting bolted firmly to the deck around which anchor cables, mooring lines or tow ropes are made fast.

SAR Search and Rescue.

Scend Vertical movement of waves or swell against, for example, a harbour wall.

Scope The ratio of the length of anchor cable let out to the depth of water.

Scupper Drain hole in the toe-rail.

Sea anchor A device, such as a conical canvas bag open at both ends, streamed from bow or stern to hold a boat bow or stern on to the wind or sea.

Sea breeze A daytime wind blowing across a coastline from the sea caused by the rising air from the heating of the land by the sun.

Sea legs The ability to keep one's feet in spite of the motion of the boat.

Seacock A stopcock next to every inlet and outlet in the hull to prevent accidental entry of water.

Searoom An area in which a vessel can navigate without difficulty or danger of hitting an obstruction.

Seaway A stretch of water where there are waves.

Securite An internationally recognised safety signal used on the radio telephone preceding an important navigational or meteorological warning.

Seize To bind two ropes together.

Serve To cover and protect a splice on a rope by binding with small line or twine.

Set (sails) To hoist a sail.

Set (tidal stream) The direction in which a tidal stream or current flows.

Set sail To start out on a voyage.

Shackle A metal link for connecting ropes, wires or chains to sails, anchors, etc. To shackle on is to connect using a shackle.

Shape A ball, cone or diamond shaped object, normally black, hoisted by day on a vessel to indicate a special state or occupation.

Sheave A wheel over which a rope or wire runs.

Sheer off To turn away from another vessel or object in the water.

Sheet Rope or line fastened to the clew of a sail or the end of the boom supporting it. Named after the sail to which it is attached.

Sheet bend A knot used to join two ropes of different size together.

Sheet in To pull in on a sheet till it is taut and the sail drawing.

Shelving A gradual slope in the seabed.

Shipping forecast Weather forecast broadcast four times each day by the British Broadcasting Corporation for the benefit of those at sea.

Shipping lane A busy track across the sea or ocean.

Shipshape Neat and efficient.

Shoal An area offshore where the water is so shallow that a ship might run aground. To shoal is to become shallow.

Shock cord Elastic rubber bands enclosed in a sheath of fibres, very useful for lashing.

Shorten in Decrease the amount of anchor cable let out.

Shorten sail To reduce the amount of sail set either by reefing or changing to a smaller sail.

Shrouds Parts of the standing rigging that support the mast laterally.

Sidedeck The deck alongside the coachroof.

Sidelight The red and green lights exhibited either side of the bows by vessels under way and making way through the water.

Sill A wall which acts as a dam, to keep water in a marina.

Siren The fog signal made by vessels over 12 metres in length when under way.

Skeg A false keel fitted near the stern which supports the leading edge of the rudder.

Skylight A framework fitted on the deck of a boat with glazed windows to illuminate the cabin and provide ventilation.

Slab reef A method of reefing a boomed sail where the sail is flaked down on top of the boom.

Slack off To ease or pay out a line.

Slack water In tidal waters, the period of time when the tidal stream is non-existent or negligible.

Slam When the underpart of the forward part of the hull hits the water when pitching in heavy seas.

Slide A metal or plastic fitting on the luff or foot of a sail running in a track on the mast or boom.

Sliding hatch A sliding hatch fitted over the entrance to the cabin.

Slip To let go quickly.

Slip lines Mooring ropes or lines doubled back so that they can be let go easily from on board.

Slipway An inclined ramp leading into the sea.

Snap hook A hook that springs shut when released.

Snap shackle A shackle that is held closed by a spring-loaded plunger.

Snarl up Lines or ropes that are twisted or entangled.

Snatch Jerk caused by too short an anchor cable in a seaway. To take a turn quickly around a cleat, bollard or samson post.

Sole The floor of a cabin or cockpit.

SOS International distress signal made by light, sound or radio.

Sound To measure the depth of water.

Sounding The depth of water below chart datum.

Spar General term for all poles used on board such as mast, boom and yard.

Speed made good The speed made good over the ground; that is, the boat speed corrected for tidal stream and leeway.

Spill wind To ease the sheets so that the sail is only partly filled by the wind, the rest being spilt.

Spindrift Fine spray blown off wave crests by strong winds.

Spinnaker A large symmetrical balloon shaped sail used when running or reaching.

Spinnaker pole A spar which is used to hold the spinnaker out.

Spit A projecting shoal or strip of land connected to the shore.

Splice A permanent join made between two ropes.

Split ring A ring like a key ring that can be fed into an eye to prevent accidental withdrawal.

Spray hood A folding canvas cover over the entrance to the cabin.

Spreaders Metal struts fitted either side of the mast to spread the shrouds out sideways.

Spring tide The tides at which the range is greatest: the height of high water is greater and that for low water is less than those for neap tides.

Springs Mooring lines fastened to prevent a boat moving forwards or backwards relative to the quay or other boats alongside.

Squall A sudden increase of wind speed often associated with a line of low dark clouds representing an advancing cold front.

Stanchions Metal posts supporting the guardrails.

Standby to gybe A warning given by the helmsman that he is about to gybe.

Stand in To head towards land.

Stand off To head away from the shore.

Stand-on vessel The boat that does not have to keep clear; it must maintain course and speed.

Standing rigging Wire rope or solid rods that support masts and fixed spars but do not control the sails.

Starboard side The right-hand side when looking forward towards the bow.

Stay Part of the standing rigging which provides support fore and aft.

Staysail A sail set on a stay.

Steady Order to the helmsman to keep the boat on her present course.

Steaming light Alternative term for masthead light.

Steep-to A sharply sloping seabed.

Steerage way A boat has steerage way when she is moving fast enough to answer to the helm; that is, to respond to deflections of the rudder.

Steering compass The compass permanently mounted adjacent to the helmsman which he uses as a reference to keep the boat on a given course.

Stem The forwardmost part of the hull.

Stemhead The top of the stem.

Stemhead fitting A fitting on the stemhead, often an anchor roller.

Stern The afterpart of the boat.

Stern gland Packing around the propeller shaft where it passes through the hull.

Stern light A white light exhibited from the stern.

Stern line The mooring line going aft from the stern.

Sternsheets The aftermost part of an open boat.

Stiff A boat that does not heel easily; opposite to tender.

Stopper knot A knot made in the end of a rope to prevent it running out through a block or fairlead.

Storm Wind of Beaufort force 10, 48 to 55 knots; or a violent storm force 11, 56 to 63 knots.

Storm jib Small heavy jib set in strong winds.

Stormbound Confined to a port or anchorage by heavy weather.

Stow Put away in a proper place. Stowed for sea implies that all gear and loose equipment has, in addition, been lashed down.

Strand To run a vessel aground intentionally or accidentally.

Strop A loop of wire rope fitted round a spar. A wire rope used to add length to the luff of a headsail.

Strum box A strainer fitted around the suction end of a bilge pump hose to prevent the pump being choked by debris.

Strut A small projecting rod.

Suit A complete set of sails.

Surge To ease a rope out round a winch or bollard.

Swashway A narrow channel between shoals.

Sweat up To tauten a rope as much as possible.

Sweep A long oar.

Swig To haul a line tight when it is under load by pulling it out at right angles and quickly taking in the slack.

Swing To rotate sideways on a mooring in response to a change in direction of the tidal stream or wind.

Swinging room The area encompassed by a swing that excludes any risk of collision or of grounding.

Synopsis A brief statement outlining the weather situation at a particular time.

Synoptic chart A weather chart covering a large area on which is plotted information giving an overall view of the weather at a particular moment.

Tack To go about from one course to another with the bow passing through the eye of the wind. A sailing boat is on a tack if she is neither gybing nor tacking.

Tack The lower forward corner of a sail.

Tackle A combination of rope and blocks designed to increase the pulling or hoisting power of a line.

Take in Lower a sail.

Take the helm Steer the boat.

Take way off To reduce the speed of the boat.

Telltales Lengths of wool or ribbon attached to the sails or shrouds to indicate the airflow or apparent direction of the wind.

Tender A boat that heels easily is said to be tender; the opposite of stiff. Also small dinghy used to take crew to a larger boat.

Thwart The athwartships seat in a small boat or dinghy.

Tidal stream The horizontal movement of water caused by the tides.

Tidal stream atlas An official publication showing the direction and rate of the tidal streams for a particular area.

Tide The vertical rise and fall of the water in the oceans in response to the gravitational forces of the sun and moon.

Tide tables Official annual publication which gives the times and heights of high and low water for standard ports and the differences for secondary ports.

Tideway The part of a channel where the tidal stream runs most strongly.

Tiller A lever attached to the rudder head by which the helmsman deflects the rudder.

Toe-rail A low strip of wood or light alloy that runs round the edge of a deck.

Toggle A small piece of wood inserted in an eye to make a quick connection.

Topping lift A line from the base of the mast passing around a sheave at the top then to the end of the boom to take the weight of the boom when lowering the sail.

Topsides The part of a boat which lies above the waterline when she is not heeled.

Track The path between two positions: ground track is that over the ground; water track is that through the water.

Traffic separation scheme In areas of heavy traffic, a system of one-way lanes. Special regulations apply to shipping in these zones.

Transceiver A radio transmitter and receiver.

Transducer A component that converts electric signals into sound waves and vice versa.

Transferred position line A position line for one time, transferred, with due allowance for the vessel's ground track, to cross with another position line at a later time.

Transit Two fixed objects are in transit when they are in line.

Transom The flat transverse structure across the stern of a hull.

Traveller The sliding car on a track, for example on the mainsheet track or adjustable headsail sheet block.

Trick Spell on duty, especially at the helm.

Tri-colour light A single light at the top of the mast of sailing boats under 20 metres long that can be used when sailing in place of the navigation lights.

Trim To adjust the sails by easing or hardening in the sheets to obtain maximum driving force.

Trip-line A line attached to the crown of an anchor to enable it to be pulled out backwards if it gets caught fast by an object on the sea-bed.

Trot Mooring buoys laid in a line.

Truck The very top of the mast.

Trysail A small heavy sail set on the mast in stormy weather in place of the mainsail.

Tune To improve the performance of a sailing boat or engine.

Twine Small line used for sewing and whipping.

Unbend To unshackle sheets and halyards and remove a sail ready to stow.

Underway A vessel is underway if it is not at anchor, made fast to the shore or aground.

Unshackle To unfasten.

Unship To remove an object from its working position.

Up and down Said of an anchor cable when it is vertical.

Uphaul A line which is used to raise a spar vertically.

Upstream The direction from which a river flows.

Upwind The direction from which the wind is blowing.

Vang A tackle or strap fitted between the boom and the toe-rail to keep the boom horizontal.

Variation The angle between the true and the magnetic meridian for any geographical position.

Veer Of a cable or line, to pay out gradually. Of the wind, to change direction clockwise.

Ventilator (vent) A fitting which allows fresh air to enter the boat.

VHF Very High Frequency; usually taken as meaning the VHF radio telephone.

Visibility The greatest distance at which an object can be seen against its background.

Wake Disturbed water left by a moving boat. The direction of the wake compared with the fore-and-aft line of the boat is often used as a rough measure of leeway.

Warp Heavy lines used for mooring, kedging or towing, and to move a boat by hauling on warps secured to a bollard or buoy.

Wash The turbulent water left astern by a moving boat.

Washboards Removable planks fitted in the cabin entrance to prevent water getting in.

Watch One of the periods into which 24 hours is divided on board.

Waterline The line along the hull at the surface of the water in which she floats.

Waypoint A navigational position stored in a GPS receiver.

Wear To change tacks by gybing.

Weather a mark To succeed in passing to windward of a mark.

Weather helm The tendency of a boat to turn her bow to windward making it necessary to hold the tiller to the weather side.

Weep To leak slowly.

Weigh anchor To raise the anchor.

Well A sump in the bilges. A small locker for the anchor.

Wheel The steering wheel that moves the rudder.

Whipping Twine bound round the ends of a rope to keep it from fraying.

Whisker pole Light spar to hold out the clew of a headsail when running, particularly when goosewinged.

Whistle An appliance to make sound signals in restricted visibility and when manoeuvring.

Winch A fitting designed to assist the crew hauling on a rope or line.

Winch handle A removable handle used for operating a winch.

Windage All parts of a boat that contribute to total air drag.

Windlass The winch used for weighing the anchor.

Windward The direction from which the wind blows.

Withies Branches used in small rivers to mark the edges of the channel.

Yankee jib A large jib set forward of the staysail in light winds.

Yard A long spar on which a square sail is set.

Yawing Swinging from side to side of the course set, or at anchor.

Yawl A two-masted boat where the mizzen mast is aft of the rudder stock.

index

accidents 107-10
aft 6
anchor winch 90
anchorages 87
anchoring 87–91
avoiding action 72–3

backstay 8
bags 2
barometers 64
battens 11
BBC shipping forecast 64
bear away 34
bearings, taking compass 52
beating 35
Beaufort wind scale 62–3
Bermudan rig 7–8, 10
berthing next to other
    boats 85
berthing, preparing for 83
blue ensign 96
boarding 4
boat parts and terms 6–11
boom 10
bowline 14
bowsprit 8
breast lines 22
briefing, skippers 4
broad reach 31
Bruce anchor 89
buoyage 44–7
    direction of 44
buoyancy aids 101
burgee 96

cable, anchor 88
cardinal marks 45
cardio-pulmonary
    resuscitation (CPR) 110
casting off 22
chain, anchor 88
channel marks 49
channels, narrow 74
chart 54–7
    corrections 57
    publishers 57
    symbols 56
cirrocumulus clouds 60
cirrostratus clouds 59
cirrus clouds 59
cleat 83
clew 10
close hauled 31, 35
clothing 2–3
clouds 59–60
coastal forecasts 65
cockpit 6
code flags 96–8
coiling rope 19
collision 106
    regulations 71–9
    risk 71
communications 115
compass 51–3
    bearings 52–3
    hand bearing 53
    rose 53
Competent Crew course
    syllabus 135
course, steering 50–3

courtesy ensign 96
CQR anchor 89
cringles 11
cumulus clouds 59, 60
cutter 7, 8

dan buoy 103
Danforth anchor 87, 89
Datascope 51
deck log 27
deck shoes 3
deviation 52
diesel engine, stopping 22
dinghy 94–5
directions from the boat 7
distress 110–15
    calls 113
    signals 110

electronic compass 51
emergencies 102–15
engine starting 21
ensign 96
environment 99
EPIRBs 114
etiquette, sailing 99

fairlead 13, 83
fenders, attaching 83, 84
fenders, positioning and
    stowing 22
figure of eight knot 14
fire 106
    blankets 106
    extinguishers 106

fighting 107
  safety 107
first aid kit 109
fisherman's bend 15
flags 96–9
flares 111–12
  safety 112
flooding, controlling 106
fog 66–7
footwear 3
foresail 8, 10

gaff-rigs 8
gales 68
galley 6
gas, using on board 107
genoa 10
getting ready to sail 20–7
gloves 3
GMDSS/DSC 113
grapnel anchor 89
gybing 33–1

halyard 9, 26
hand bearing compass 53
hanking on headsail 27
harbour, entering 80–5
harbour, mooring alongside
  84, 85
harness 2, 100
hats 3
head injuries 108
headsail 10
  hoisting 26
  lowering 82
  reefing 41
heaving a line 19
heeling 34
helicopter rescue 115
hitches 14, 15
HM Coastguard 65
hoisting sails 24–7
house flag 96
hypothermia 107

injuries 108

in-mast reefing 41
inshore waters forecast 64–5
isolated danger marks 47

jammers 25
jib 10

kedge anchor 91
ketch 7, 8
kicking strap 9
knot terms 16
knots 14–15

lateral marks 44
latitude 55
leaving a raft of boats 23
leaving the boat 85
lee shore 41, 68
leech 10, 26
leeward 34
lifejacket 2, 100–1
liferafts 104–5
lift 29
light characteristics 49
lights and shapes 75–9
line, heaving a 19
lines, stowing 22
longitude 55
lookout, keeping a 24, 71
lowering sails 81
lowering the anchor 88–90
luff 10, 25
luff up 34

mainsail 10
mainsail,
  hoisting 25–6
  lowering 81
  stowing 81, 82
mainsheet 9, 26
man overboard 102–4
marinecall 64
Mayday 113
MCA boat identification
  scheme 105
medical assistance 114

medicines, personal 4
meridians of latitude and
  longitude 55
mooring 92–3
mooring lines 22, 83
mooring, leaving 92

narrow channels 74
nautical miles 55
nautical publications 57
Navtex 65, 66
no sail sector 31
nylon rope 12

orange smoke signals 111

parts of a rope 13
parts of the boat 6–11
picking up a man overboard
  103–4
picking up a mooring 92, 93
points of sailing 30
points reefing 39
pole 8
poling out the headsail 31
polyester rope 12
polypropylene rope 12
pontoon, mooring to 84
port side 6
port hand marks 44, 45
preparing the boat 20
preventer 34
pulpit 9
push pit 9
pyrotechnics 111–12

raft of boats, leaving 23
reach 31, 35
recovery position 110
red hand-held flare 111
red parachute flare 112
reef knot 14
reefing 11, 36–41
  headsail 41
  in-mast 41
  points 39

roller 38, 40
slab 38, 40
resuscitation 109
riding turns on a winch 18
risk of collision 71
rock, symbols on charts 56
roller reefing 38, 40
rolling hitch 15
rope types 12
rope, coiling 19
rope, parts of 13
ropework 12–20
rough seas sailing 36–7
round turn and two half
   hitches 14
rules of the road 71–9
running 31, 36
running rigging 9

safe water marks 47
safety 100–1
   equipment 4
   in fog 67
sail trim 30
sailing cruiser, parts of 8–9
sailing terms 34
sailing theory 28–41
sailing upwind 32
sails 10
   hoisting 24–7
   lowering 81

SART 115
scarves 3
schooner 7, 8
sectored lights 48
self-jamming cleats 16
self-tailing winch 17
sheave 25
sheet bend 15
sheet, releasing 18
shock 108
shore lights 48
shrouds 8, 25
slab reefing 38, 40
slip lines 22
sloop 7
smoke signals 111
sound signals 79
spar 8
special marks 47
spinnaker 36
spreaders 25
stanchions 9
standing rigging 8
starboard 6
starboard hand marks 44, 45
steering 30
stern 6
storm jib 10
stowing lines 22
stowing the mainsail 81
sunglasses 3

symbols, chart 56
synthetic ropes, care of 13

tack (sail corner) 11
tacking 32
telltales 36
topmarks on buoys 45
topping lift 9, 26
traffic separation scheme 74
transits 48
traveller 25
trip line on anchor 91
types of rope 12

urgency calls (Pan Pan)
   113–14

variation 52
VHF radio 113

waterproof clothing 2–3
weather 58–69
Weather fax 66
weather forecasts 64
weather side 34
weighing anchor 90
white hand held flare 112
winching 16–18
wind indicator 64
withies 46
wreck marker buoy 47